THINKING CHILDREN

Debating Play Series

Series Editor: Tina Bruce

The intention behind the 'Debating Play' series is to encourage readers to reflect on their practices so that they are in a position to offer high-quality play opportunities to children. The series will help those working with young children and their families in diverse ways and contexts, to think about how to cultivate early childhood play with rich learning potential.

The 'Debating Play' series examines cultural myths and taboos. It considers matters of human rights and progress towards inclusion in the right to play for children with complex needs. It looks at time-honoured practices and argues for the removal of constraints on emergent play. It challenges readers to be committed to promoting play opportunities for children traumatized by war, flight, violence and separation from loved ones. It draws upon crucial contemporary research that demonstrates how children in different parts of the world develop their own play culture in ways that help them make sense of their lives.

Published and forthcoming titles:

Forbes: *Beginning to Play*
Holland: *We Don't Play With Guns Here*
Hyder: *War, Conflict and Play*
Kalliala: *Play Culture in a Changing World*
Manning-Morton and Thorp: *Key Times for Play*
Orr: *My Right to Play: A Child with Complex Needs*
Tovey: *Playing Outdoors*

THINKING CHILDREN

LEARNING ABOUT SCHEMAS

Anne Meade and Pam Cubey

 Open University Press

Open University Press
McGraw-Hill Education
McGraw-Hill House
Shoppenhangers Road
Maidenhead
Berkshire
England
SL6 2QL

email: enquiries@openup.co.uk
world wide web: www.openup.co.uk

and
Two Penn Plaza, New York, NY 10121-2289, USA

First published Open University Press 2008

A catalogue record of this book is available from the British Library

ISBN10: 0 335 22880 1 (pb)   0335 22879 8 (hb)
ISBN13: 978 0 335 22880 5 (pb)   978 0335 22879 9 (hb)

Library of Congress Cataloging-in-Publication Data
CIP data has been applied for

Typeset by RefineCatch Limited, Bungay, Suffolk
Printed in Great Britain by Bell and Bain Ltd., Glasgow

Fictitous names of companies, products, people, characters and/or data that may be used herein (in case studies or in examples) are not intended to represent any real individual, company, product or event.

Thinking Children was first published by the New Zealand Council for Educational Research (NZCER Press) 1995.

The **McGraw·Hill** Companies

To Tina Bruce who introduced us to Chris Athey, and to Chris Athey herself – through their work on the Froebel Early Education project, and subsequent writing, countless teachers and parents have gained invaluable insights into young children's thinking.

CONTENTS

LIST OF FIGURES AND TABLES

Figures

Photos

Tables

ACKNOWLEDGEMENTS

There are many people we would like to thank for their help as we revised this book. The Wilton Playcentre members have been very supportive, especially the families of the six case study children in Chapter 5. Most of the photos are from the Wilton Playcentre collections, and Rebecca Bulman provided expertise with accessing the photos. Conversations with Linda Mitchell and Nikolien van Wijk have stretched our thinking about children's schema learning, and Nikolien made helpful comments on the draft manuscript.

Valda Kirkwood, an academic colleague and friend, gave valuable professional and personal feedback.

A Fulbright Senior Scholarship in 1999 enabled Anne Meade to study the development of young children's minds and brains, which has been put to good use in this first English edition of *Thinking Children*.

Little, Brown Book Group has granted non-exclusive, print-only World English language extract rights to use the words from *Rosetta* by Barbara Ewing quoted in Chapter 5.

Copyright permission has been given by Chris Athey, Tina Bruce and Cathy Nutbrown to use all the quotes we have included from their respective books. Copyright permission has also been given for the use of material originating from the New Zealand Ministry of Education cited in *Thinking Children* (2nd edn.).

PREFACE

I have wanted this book to be available to a wider readership for some time. The original edition, published in New Zealand, was very well received and it is timely to introduce this revised edition now. Anne Meade and Pam Cubey are deeply respected and well known early childhood experts in New Zealand and internationally.

The subject of children thinking is a time honoured one. The intellectual life of children can be the difference between fulfilled lives or lives that are lacking the possibilities for creativity, reflection, the curiosity that goes with problem seeking and problem solving, the place of surprise, or confirmation. Thinking is an emotional business, and part of the way children make relationships.

In this book, readers will meet particular children and practitioners, and see their thinking in action. The focus is on the way the brain develops schemas which enable deep and effective learning as the child develops and relates to people, physical and cultural experiences. The book makes difficult theory very accessible, and is never divorced from practical day to day experiences of working with young children.

I am delighted that the authors agreed to write this book, incorporating recent work they have been involved in, and using up to date theory in very easy to read ways. It makes a contribution to the field of work on schemas, encouraging observation that informs practice and helps children to get more out of life. It also helps practitioners and parents to enjoy the time they spend with their children, and to gain insights into how to help them flourish in their development and learning.

Tina Bruce
Series Editor

1

RESEARCHING SCHEMAS

Chapter 1 introduces schemas and schema learning, situating this work within constructivist theory. In the latter part of the chapter, the two research projects used in the book are introduced: the Competent Children action research study, and the Wilton Playcentre centre of innovation project. The aims, research processes, early childhood centres and families in the two research projects are described. A plan of the book completes the chapter.

'As adults, we see different things': on Nina, spiral spotter

Nina's mother wrote:

> One day, Nina went off to Kindergarten as usual. Nina was Nina. By the afternoon, she was a different girl: Nina, spiral spotter. During the day she had been playing with her friend Katie, the overhead projector and some round coloured glass circles. When they projected it onto the ceiling, a spiral shone down on them from above and the spell was cast. Nina was on a mission. There was a job to be done and six months later there still is. There probably always will be because there seem to be spirals everywhere. 'Look, that candle holder is a spiral.' 'My violin has a spiral on the end.' 'Your earrings are spirals.' 'Grace's hair curls into spirals, I'll have to take it to morning meeting.' No!!
>
> Everywhere we go there are spirals. As adults, we seem to see different things. We saw a fly screen; Nina saw wrought-iron spiral designs in the frame. Ditto for a fancy letterbox [near] our place. The billboard advertisement on the way to school: 'Look

Mum, there are spirals on your legs!' I hadn't realised the pattern on my tights had spirals. Nina doesn't miss things – her eyes light up and she gets very excited when she spots a spiral. She has really developed her observation skills since noticing spirals.

The other amazing aspect of this business of 'spirals on the brain' is how it leads to further activities and thoughts. . . . The design on the box of tissues has spirals, but 'they forgot to put spirals on the tissues'. So out come the [pens]. Nina's drawing has changed since spirals. . . . It's something to do with starting a spiral from a centre and then it not having to end, so she can keep on going with it. She's done spiral maps and houses and pathways, which began as spirals and end up as something else.

(Liljegren n.d.)

Introduction ∎

This book is about 'spirals' and other schemas 'on the brain'. As adults, we get 'tunes on the brain', particularly from our childhood. It is usually a musical phrase, not the complete song or symphony, which pops back into our consciousness – it is a musical schema (see later definitions). There are many and varied memories in the form of schemas stored in our subconscious mind, also known as implicit memories. They are different from memories of events or facts, or from our autobiographical memories. These forms of thought have significance in understanding the world around us.

There are 'jobs to be done' in relation to schema learning, particularly for the young. When adults support those 'jobs being done', and the lines of thinking leading from them, children's thinking is enriched. According to Nina's mother:

Nina found an advertisement for New Zealand on a magazine cover. An old Māori man's face is painted with a beautiful intricate spiral design which made Nina wonder about how he put it on and what 'tradition' means and where New Zealand is. He is touching noses with a young child as a form of greeting, so discussion switches to kissing.

(Liljegren n.d.)

Schema fascinations remind us that learning has biological as well as social aspects. The brain's ability to process information – to capture, store and retrieve information in circuits of connected brain cells – is what makes learning possible.

Two action research projects in New Zealand, carried out 10 years apart, provide insights into the value of schema learning theory for learning and teaching in early childhood education. They provide most of the information and illustrations about schema learning in this book.

What are schemas?   ■

Schemas are a form of thought that relate to cognitive structures. They are like pieces of ideas or concepts. Patterns in children's actions, or in their drawings and paintings, indicate common themes or threads (schemas) of thinking running through them.

'Schemas' is the term Piaget gave to cognitive structures that have been developed by individuals internalizing their actions and content in the environment. He believed that 'thought consists of internalised and co-ordinated action schemas' (Piaget 1959: 357–86). Athey defined a schema as 'a pattern of repeatable behaviour into which experiences are assimilated and that are gradually coordinated. Coordinations lead to higher-level and more powerful schemas' ([1990]; 2007: 50).

Athey ([1990]; 2007: 48) says that in 1969 Piaget clarified and made a distinction between 'schemes' (operative, a scheme of action) and 'schemas' (figural thought). Most contemporary writers conflate the two: 'A schema is a pattern of action as well as a pattern for action' (Neisser 1976, cited in Athey [1990]; 2007: 48). At times, we keep them separate.

Bruce says that 'there are two paths of a child's development: the biological path and the socio-cultural path'. Schemas have both aspects.

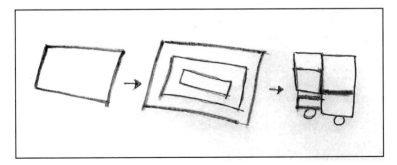

Figure 1.1 Repeated drawings of oblongs, becoming more complex.

- *Biological aspects*   A baby is born with a repertoire of schemas that are biologically predetermined and that, as they mature, coordinate, integrate, transform and ripple out into evermore complex and sophisticated forms.
- *Socio-cultural aspects*   The socio-cultural aspects of schemas are to do with the way that experience, as opposed to biological maturation, influences the development of schemas through childhood and also through our adult lives. Because the two are in a perpetual state of interaction, each influences the other, causing changes, modifications and transformations in the ways we think, feel, move and relate to others.

(Bruce 2005: 72)

Elsewhere, one of the authors, Anne Meade (2001), has written about the neurobiological bases of children's learning and development. An extract is shown below to explain more about the biological and socio-cultural aspects of schemas.

Memory is composed of multiple separate systems, which associate with different abilities. Important categories of memory systems include:

- the short-term memory (also known as working memory) and long-term memory system;
- the conscious (explicit) memory and unconscious (implicit) memory system;
- memory for events and autobiographical narrative memory.

Each of these has a different brain organization. Larry Squire states that explicit memory covers facts and events, while implicit memory includes skills and habits (Meade 2001: 67). Implicit memories include all the learned skills and behaviours that we are no longer aware of. In childhood, or sometime in the past, they become habitual because of a lot of practice.

> Early experience can affect subsequent behaviour, but the mechanism by which experience persists does not include a record of the event itself. Behaviour simply changes. Thus, following multiple and varied encounters, experience can result in altered dispositions, preferences, conditioned responses, habits and skills, but these changes do not afford any potential for an awareness that behaviour is being influenced by past experience.
>
> (Squire 1995, cited in Meade 2001: 17)

Implicit memories are acquired and stored from an early age. We argue that this is where much learning derived from play is stored. Implicit memories include perceptual, bodily 'know-how' forms of memories and schemas.

During their earliest years, children are 'coming to know' more about different schemas through their perception and actions:

> As a result of applying a range of action schemas to objects, infants arrive at the generalisations that objects are 'throwable', 'suckable' and bangable'. An infant may perform one schema on a range of objects, or a wide variety of schemas on one object.
>
> (Foss 1974, cited in Athey [1990] 2007: 49–50)

By the age of 3 or 4, they can think about schemas in the abstract. The two principal observable ways younger children 'come to know' are by using symbolic representation (for example painting and language), and exploring through action.

We argue that biological and socio-cultural aspects interact as follows. First encounters with natural objects or cultural artefacts go into short-term memory storage. Young children explore things in many different ways; they are genetically equipped to seek novelty. Gradually they work out patterns in their experiences with people and things. The patterns learned through their multiple and varied encounters (perceptual and/or bodily) result in the synapses between brain cells being strengthened. Implicit memories or schemas have been created. When other people make children more aware of those implicit memories through social interactions, some of these unconscious memories transform into conscious memories. Where schema awareness is promoted by adults who are mindful of possible schemas, it is likely to connect with children's autobiographical narrative and have positive dispositional consequences. Memory for events associated with adults enriching schema learning will support implicit memories becoming explicit too.

The Froebel Early Education researcher, Chris Athey ([1990] 2007) observed 20 children daily for two years (from age 3 to age 5). The patterns in their creations and explorations indicated when children were working on or with particular schemas. Chris and the teacher, Tina Bruce, found that young children progress to thinking about schemas using symbolic representation in the visual arts before they demonstrate their thoughts through language alone and in different timeframes by recalling past actions during conversations.

The Froebel project found that all the children made systematic advances in *forms of thought* (schemas or concepts). The data showed that when children progressed to abstract thinking, they brought both their forms of thought – their schemas – and content knowledge from earlier learning. These advances in schematic thinking and in knowing 'stuff' (content) were assisted by the adults creating more opportunities for the children to extend their range of relevant experiences. According to Athey ([1990: 138] 2007), 'With all schemas, paucity or richness of experience becomes increasingly apparent with age'.

The authors of this book argue in favour of a wealth of opportunities to give children varying encounters with 'fragments' of information that consolidate their schemas. Then these schemas combine in different ways as the 'complete set of information' needed for understanding a particular concept. Graham Nuthall's (2007) detailed research on students' learning experiences shows that these concepts do not become long-term memories until the students encounter the complete set of coordinated schemas at least three times.

> There is a certain amount of information that a student needs in order to understand [a] concept. . . . A student might experience this information in a variety of different ways, or in a variety of different parts or fragments.
>
> We discovered that a student needed to encounter, on at least three different occasions, the complete set of information she or he needed to understand the concept.
>
> (Nuthall 2007: 63)

An example is the Froebel project, where records indicated that by the age of 3 one child, Alistair, was strongly pursuing the movement schema involving 'circular direction and rotation'. The teachers and his parents were keen to keep active and to nourish his demonstrated interest in 'rotation'.

Motor level

> Alistair (3 years 9 months), on a visit to the Science Museum, could not be moved from a mechanical model of a man rotating a handle, which turned a large wooden handle screw in order to winch water from the well.

Symbolic representation

> Alistair (3 years 9 months) [made] 'A car with wheels'. He made the wheels go round and said, 'Look, they go round.' He then pointed to square shapes on top (seats) and said, 'And they go round.' He had been absorbed by the typist's chair.

Figure 1.2 Circular direction and rotation.

Functional dependency (between 'rotation' and another schema)

Alistair (4 years 9 months), following a visit to the railway, worked with Jack. They made a level crossing. They set up the railway track, intersected with a road ['grid' schema]. They closed the level-crossing gates by 'rotating' them so that they closed off the road. . . . They made the train go along the tracks. They 'rotated' the gates back again, and made the cars move across the railway line.

Thought level

Alistair (3 years 6 months) noted the effect on wet clothes of 'turning' the handle of a mangle. His mother encouraged him by suggesting he reversed the direction. . . . [Later], Alistair started a conversation with his father about a fishing rod. He said, 'You know a fishing rod? When you throw it out [he made an enactive gesture of casting the line] the string goes right out.' His mother asked, 'What happens when you reverse the rotation of the handle?' Alistair said, 'The line gets shorter'.

(Athey 1990: 139–41)

This example also illustrates how the adults were deliberately using language to enhance children's understanding of schemas. They also consolidated his mathematical learning by asking, 'What happens when . . .?'

Athey's second edition ([1990] 2007) demonstrates progressions that have continuity, whereby clusters of schemas form (coordinate) as concepts with real-world applications. For example, Alistair coordinates vertical and circular trajectories.

> Alistair (4 years 1 month) made a model of 'A train on a track'. He pointed to part of the model and said, 'That's where you wait and it goes round'. His mother said teasingly, 'I've never seen a platform go round'. Alistair said firmly, 'Well, this one does'.

> . . . Alistair was applying his 'rotation' schema with abandon. His mother was trying to wean him away from the idea of a rotating platform because she viewed it as a wrong idea and, as far as Alistair's intentions were concerned, she was probably right. When Mrs B (the teacher) and the present writer pointed out that such things existed . . . for reversing trains, Alistair was not only absorbed, he was jubilant and triumphant.
>
> (Athey [1990] 2007: 178)

The way children think about *static schemas* starts simple and becomes complex. For instance, children think about things such as 'vertical' and want to know about the properties that define 'vertical' – a schema that is very dominant in physical structures in our world. They also become fascinated with more advanced or more complex *action schemas* such as 'dynamic vertical' seen in trajectory experiments and exploration of the science of gravity.

Constructivism ∎

Both Tina Bruce (the teacher) and Chris Athey (the researcher) involved in the Froebel Project on schema learning describe their approach as constructivist. They believe that individuals construct their thinking, but differ from Jean Piaget in showing that adult enrichments (social constructions) build cognitive structures and therefore learning.

Teachers who are consciously working within a social constructivist approach want to 'extend children's thinking with worthwhile curriculum content' (Athey [1990] 2007: 36), and are continually planning possible ways to do this so that they are ready to respond at the moments when children approach 'zones of proximal development'. Alistair's teacher and mother did this.

Constructivists emphasize the development of knowledge and understanding ahead of dispositional learning (which is currently dominant in New Zealand). Constructivist teachers want to advance the learners' intellectual development. Those focusing on dispositional learning concentrate on children's positive attitudes to learning, for example, being curious. (The focuses are not unrelated; they are a matter of emphasis.)

Constructivists are interested in the processes by which children construct their own knowledge and understanding. Listening to children is central to their pedagogy. However, constructivist teachers consider not only what the children bring to the learning situation in an early years setting from other experiences, but they also consider what they want to add in order to help advance understanding. Thus, they observe children's actions and talk; they assess children's meaning-making and create new learning experiences that will take children from a state of lesser knowledge to more complete or complex understanding. They think a lot about the processes by which the ideas being explored by the children could develop and be developed. The processes under the spotlight include tapping internal thinking processes of the children, as well as pedagogical processes. Listening closely and thinking about their role in fostering learning mean that the teacher also learns and changes.

Experienced constructivist teachers know that many children of a similar age will share similar conceptual concerns; for example 4-year-olds are fascinated by death and dying, animate and inanimate objects. During periods when children express common interests, and have a high motivation to learn more about these concepts, the constructivist teacher will create opportunities for children to encounter the concept and explore it in groups. That is, constructivist teachers do not limit 'advancement of thought' to one-to-one situations. They arrange 'encounters' for groups of children to bump up against alternate views – usually in enjoyable ways – to prompt individuals to accommodate one or more alternatives into his or her existing cognitive structure (schema). Accommodation can be prompted too by changing the environment, which may or may not provoke discussion.

The aims of the teachers are to help children to:

- see the connection between the new experience and their prior knowledge;
- experience additional views about a schema or concept;
- build shared knowledge in social situations;

- find some interest and relevance in new experience, and thereby
- help shift the concept from their working memories to their long-term memories.

Constructivist teachers have an interactionist view of children. They want the learner to speculate and be active in constructing their knowledge and understanding. They expect that of themselves too. Inquiry and experiments are encouraged, rather than expecting children to accept information unthinkingly. The emphasis is on child-initiated activity, and children completing tasks at their own pace. Social and physical environments are organized to support this. The role of the educator is to facilitate learning, not to instruct.

Views of the child ■

Bruce (2005) states that the most typical lenses used to view the child are:

> **The empiricist lens.** Looking through this lens, the child is seen as an empty vessel to be filled or a lump of clay to be moulded by adults into the desired shape. This derives from the philosophy of John Locke (1632–1704).
> **The nativist lens.** This is the opposite of the empiricist approach. The nativist practitioner sees the child as pre-programmed to unfold in certain directions. This is influenced by the philosopher Jean-Jacques Rousseau (1712–1778).
> **The interactionist view.** Children are seen partly as empty vessels and partly pre-programmed. There is an interaction within and between the two. Immanuel Kant (1724–1804) originated this [view].
>
> (2005: 2)

Behaviourism is similar to empiricism. Behaviourists argue that learning is determined by the physical environment and social conditioning. Well-known behaviourists were John Watson (1878–1958) and B.F. Skinner (1904–1990). Behaviourists believe that differences in children's (or adults') skills and knowledge emanate from the opportunities they have had to learn [memorize] them, to 'fill the vessel', and from adults' reinforcement of that learning; in other words, they hold that nurture and culture determine learning. Moreover, their main aim is to transfer content knowledge. Their approaches cannot foster critical thinking and creativity.

Another term for seeing children through a nativist lens, and driven by *nature* and their genes, is 'maturationism'. Arnold Gesell (1880–1961) believed that each child has an individual temperament and growth style, and she or he matures via pre-programmed orderly sequence of stages. Some people mistakenly think Jean Piaget was a maturationist. This was not the case. For Piaget, 'stages' was a classification system – with the stages representing increasingly comprehensive ways of thinking.

The interactionists view children as being active learners. Key thinkers include Jean Piaget, Lev Vygotsky, John Dewey, Jerome Bruner and Chris Athey.

These theorists hold that all learners individually and/or collectively learn through actions that result in taking in information, linking it with what is known already and/or working with it in order to turn it into new understandings. The nature part of the interaction equation is the existence and development of mental structures. Knowledge is constructed within. Direct experience of the world is regarded as very important for constructing new understandings. Social constructivists emphasize the importance of other humans for learning, especially more expert others. Jerome Bruner is described as sitting somewhere between Piaget and Vygotsky, between the individual and social constructivists. 'Like Piaget, he emphasizes action and problem-solving in children's learning, but, like Vygotsky, he stresses the importance of social interaction, language and instruction in the development of thinking' (Robson 2006: 31).

Bruner argues that abstract, logical thought is not the one and only goal for learning and development. He explores three categories of representation:

- enactive representation: action-based representation;
- iconic representation: in pictures or images of things;
- symbolic representation: when learners use language or mathematical symbols to represent their thinking.

Bruner is well known for his metaphor of scaffolding learning (Bruner 1971). Scaffolding involves engaging the child's interest, then guiding his or her activities, and praising effort, in order to help the learner become consciously in control of the action or concept being learned.

Pedagogical approaches

Different pedagogical approaches can be used by educators as circumstances vary. The main pedagogical approach in an educational

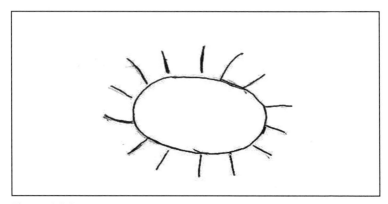

Figure 1.3 Iconic representation.

setting, however, will follow from the view of the child that dominates. The view of the child colours the teachers' thinking about learning and teaching, and about organizing the environment.

Educators who adhere to empiricist or behaviourist views of the child think that the adult should control or lead all the learning. Direct instruction dominates in these early childhood settings. Educators control the use of time and space, set goals for children's learning and direct children through a step-by-step programme so that the intended learning is covered. Adults believe they know best and set the content. They provide a lot of self-correcting teaching materials, and open-ended materials are less evident.

In contrast, nativist or developmental maturationist teachers exercise relatively loose control. They observe the child to identify where she or he is on a sequence of stages of development, then they set up the environment to facilitate learning associated with the stage of 'normal development'. For example, Maria Montessori espouses the importance of preparing a series of activities structured to the children's needs and the importance of minimal interference from adults. The role of nativist teachers is to lay 'stepping stones' and allow the child to lead his or her own learning. Even though children are relatively free to decide how they use time and space, and to follow their own interests, the adults are expected to guide children to conform to the scientific views of normal behaviour for their stage of development.

Bruce says interactionism is 'a little like having conversations, dancing together or making music together' (2005: 5). She was referring to 'dances' between nature and nurture. Neuroscientists who focus on child development – and who join this broad group – use similar metaphors. One neuroscientist suggests an 'overlapping waves' model of learning (Siegler 2000). These metaphors indicate that processes are emphasized ahead of content.

The constructivist (interactionist) approach will involve, at times, children leading processes for constructing new knowledge (on their own or in groups) and, at other times, adults guiding. Children will be afforded many opportunities to learn by doing, and to interact with the environment, especially through play. Unstructured time and access to a rich array of materials is important for both socio-cultural learning and for individual constructivism. Time and space are organized loosely to facilitate children's active exploration and theorizing about people, places and things. Sharing thoughts and feelings is expected as adults join children as co-learners and/or problem-posers. Educators need to decide on what support to offer, how specific they will be and the timing of their guidance.

Content emanates from individual or group interest, and is presented in a holistic way, for example, through projects. Constructivists aim to enable the advancement of learners' intellectual development often through projects that last for days or weeks.

An introduction to the two research projects ■

The two action research projects used in this book are the Competent Children action research study, and the Wilton Playcentre centre of innovation project. Both provide insights into the value of schema learning theory for learning and teaching in early childhood education. Both sets of educators supported children as they identified, then worked with different schemas that were 'on children's brains', and extended their thinking. The teachers and parents helped children keep on going when their eyes lit up about particular schemas, like spirals, grids, and so on. They provided additional socio-cultural experiences relevant for the consolidation of those schemas in the brain.

The first project was part of an ongoing longitudinal study, known as the Competent Children project, to look at the effects of early childhood contexts on children's development. It focused on the question, 'What experiences influence the development of children's competencies?' Ministry of Education funding of the establishment phase of the project allowed the research team to carry out a small action research study in 1993, at the same time as they piloted some of the instruments for the longitudinal study. The purpose of the action research study, which is reported here, was to examine the effects on children's learning of intervening in their curriculum at home and in early childhood settings, by heightening adults' awareness of schema development. Teachers, parents and researchers participating in this study agreed to incorporate practices derived from schema development theories into their curricula to enhance children's cognitive development.

The second action research study was carried out between 2003 and 2006, by the Wilton Playcentre, a Ministry of Education designated centre of innovation. Of interest in this book was their inclusion of schemas. This second study was also designed to heighten parent educators' awareness of children's schema interests and to extend that learning through a range of practices. As the educators were also parents of the enrolled children, the schema learning passed between centre and the home, as well as between generations.

We were involved in both projects, although our roles changed. We found too that our thinking had moved forward over the decade, as had other scholars writing about schemas, such as Chris Athey and Cathy Nutbrown.

The Competent Children action research study ■

The main aims of the wider Competent Children study are to describe the progress of 500 children over time, and to chart the contributions to their progress made by: family resources, early childhood education, school experiences, children's activities in the home or outside school, and relationships with other children. When the children were approaching 5 years old, data were gathered about the children's early development, formal early childhood care and education, and family background, as well as about aspects of the early childhood service they were attending. Before they started school, an assessment of several competencies was made.

The Competent Children sub-study focused on six months in the lives of nine children between 4 and 5 years old who were fortunate to have their teachers (at least the staff in their early childhood centres and most parents) tune in to their exploration and thinking about mathematical and science-related schemas. (Schema research is predominantly about mathematical and science schemas.) As we will show in the Wilton Playcentre project, literacy-related schemas can also be studied.

Chapter 4 also provides findings about another eight children who were chosen as comparison subjects. The 17 children attended four early childhood centres in the Wellington region. All 17 children were also included in the total sample for the main Competent

Children project and were included in the analyses for the qualitative study.

The aims of the action research sub-study were to:

- introduce staff and parents of nine children to the theory of schema development and the findings of the Froebel Early Education project, and to provide them with resources about schemas;
- assist staff with, and foster observations of, children's work on schemas evident in children's art and other representations, and children's talk, and children's actions;
- foster curriculum innovations by staff to facilitate children's development of schemas;
- document these children's development of competencies, alongside that of peers in similar early childhood settings and compared with all the children involved in the quantitative component of the Competent Children project at later stages of the longitudinal study.

The approach taken

The action research study within the Competent Children project was designed so that the teachers (and the researchers) 'could learn from their own experience and make this experience accessible to others' (McTaggart 1989: 1). Features of action research included:

- the teachers (and the researchers) were committed to improvement;
- those affected by the hoped-for changes had primary responsibility for making the decisions about what curriculum and/or pedagogical changes to make;
- the teachers developed new understandings of pedagogy that extended and refined their work.

Where it differed from some other action research studies was:

- the changes did not start from the teachers perceiving a practical issue that could be resolved by a process of collecting data and developing a theoretical analysis of the experiences they had;
- the participants in the research – the teachers, parents and children – had little say about the design of the study, although the adults had reasonable control over the ways they observed and recorded children's behaviour.

The Competent Children project team identified two centres that met the selection criteria. Key staff members were asked whether they would like to participate in a curriculum innovation, revolving around schema development. The staff were interested, consulted internally (which is important for action research), then consented.

The researchers approached the research believing that adults can enhance the possibilities for, and from, children's active exploration of schemas or 'threads of thinking' (Nutbrown [1994] 2006). To do this, the researchers wanted the teachers to:

- identify, reflect on, plan for and talk about the children's schemas at staff programme planning meetings;
- during sessions, help children recall experiences that link into their current strand of thinking, talk about the representations of that schema evident in, say, the children's paintings in ways which would extend their language and thinking about that schema;
- provide a rich environment for the children to explore, at the centre and on excursions into the community;
- talk to parents so that they too could provide opportunities for further learning following the same 'thread of thought'.

It should be emphasized that the researchers were not encouraging teacher-imposed themes; indeed, the chances are such themes would not fulfil the children's need for continuing their own threads of thinking. Nor were they seeking lots of change in the centre environments, only variations in content over time as well as more adult–child talk, in keeping with the need to nourish individual children's schema learning.

Almost all changes to the curriculum were in the hands of the teachers. Once a child's interest in a particular schema was spotted, they were left with the primary responsibility for deciding what changes to make to extend the learning.

Introducing schema theory to the participants

The action researcher ran workshops for staff at the two intervention centres, explaining Athey's research findings about schemas ([1990] 2007). The workshop covered different types of *action schemas* (in the sense of repeated patterns of action) and the researcher showed a video of two children, one of whom was absorbed in an action schema ('trajectory', squirting water, where her fascination became more intense as she engaged in scientific experimentation and found that the trajectory altered as the water pressure changed). Written materials were handed out with examples of children's work to assist in spotting *figurative schema* in drawings, paintings and models.

Photo 1.1 Rosa's hose trajectory.

About 10 days later, the researcher visited the centres again to do some running record observations of the 10 target children and to talk to staff about any schemas they had detected. Two weeks later, she ran a workshop for the target children's parents and some staff. The parents were immediately able to identify with some of the schema examples. They too were given written materials to assist their recognition of a range of schemas and asked to take note of further examples. After six weeks, a follow-up workshop was held for staff from both intervention centres on the schemas they had observed and on sharing assessment records.

The action researcher's field notes provided some insights into the difficulties of schema spotting.

It was much more difficult to spot the schemas than I had imagined. Although I observed the children closely and carried out running records on my visits, and staff made independent observations, conclusions about schemas could be only tentative in the first weeks. 'Enclosure', 'enveloping', and 'connecting' [action] schemas seemed easier to identify than some others. It is difficult in a session to pick out repeated patterns of behaviour for several children. It was only when the observations had accumulated, that there was some confidence in associating certain schemas with the children.

(Cubey, December 1993)

Later, with more practice, schema 'spotting' became much easier for the researcher and teachers.

Curriculum interventions

Curriculum innovations that extend learning can occur in the curriculum *content* or curriculum *processes* or both, usually preceded by sharpening observations. For instance, one child Paul was fascinated by 'containing', 'going through' and 'going around'. Staff provided him with a range of different materials. With these additional resources, he 'contained' and 'went around' his wrists with some sewing tape, he passed streamers through several doorways ('going through' boundaries) and tied them ('going around') to furniture in each room, and he wrapped parcels with string. Staff and parents exchanged anecdotes about Paul working on this schema daily.

In an example of changing the curriculum process, teachers in one centre noticed that several children were exploring 'containment' – they were frequently filling buckets of sand or gathering fallen leaves into a bucket. One teacher offered soup-making as an extension activity and the target children helped to cut a carrot and put it inside the pot for cooking the soup. The adult supported the schema learning by using language such as 'inside the pot' and 'inside the soup'.

Most teachers will say that there was nothing particularly innovative about these curriculum and pedagogical approaches to nourish the children's learning. This is true – they applied their usual strategies for extending learning. What was different was these teachers were noticing that the children's interest in buckets had a schematic core to it – it was not just random behaviour; and their interest was not about buckets *per se*. The teachers could have intervened by introducing pretend play with buckets that had nothing to do with a containment schema, but they did not. Instead, they recognized that children were experimenting to learn more about containment, and were accumulating mathematical and scientific knowledge in the process about how quantities within the same container can vary according to the properties of different materials. The teachers had sharpened their observation skills, tuned in differently via children's schema interests and responded by providing a different experience for children to continue their thinking about containment – soup in a container with ingredients that have different properties. The teachers had become more aware of the patterns of children's thinking and doing (their schemas). This in itself is a significant development. They responded by offering the children a new experience that was more complex, as it involved mixing different materials in a container. The teachers' thinking about how to add complexity was also a significant development.

Data collection

Three sets of people were involved in observing the children to try and ascertain schemas that might be dominant in their exploration and thinking during the two terms' participation in the action research: staff at the centres, the researcher and the parents of the children. The staff were asked to help in two ways: keeping event records and compiling schema data from existing assessment documentation.

The staff: event sampling

First, to maintain a *wall chart* about the children, keeping a brief record of actions, representations or language that illustrated particular schema. This type of observation is called 'event recording'. The staff jotted a brief note on a 'yellow sticky' and attached it to the chart. Before long, in one centre, staff had identified several schemas of interest to children at around age 4. After a period, the chart began to resemble a graph (see Figure 1.4).

The staff: records of target children

Second, staff were asked to compile data on each child's schemas using current records as far as possible. One centre already had a

	Child A	Child B	Child C	Child D
Vertical dynamic	**			
Trajectory			**	****
Connecting		***	*	**
Going around a boundary (etc.)				***

Figure 1.4 Staff records of schemas.

home book system of recording photos of the children and observation notes in a book for parents to read and add to. Material about schemas was included in those books. The other centre had a system of making books for each child large enough to include some paintings, and they adapted this for the research.

The action researcher

She undertook the action research field work and visited each centre at least once a month in order to discuss progress on spotting schemas and ideas for nourishing them. Her data collection comprised *running records*. She observed each child two to three times for 15–20-minute intervals on each visit, carefully described what he or she was doing, and added notes about the context as appropriate. At a later stage, she coded the observational records of *graphic* and *action representations* or the language that indicated a particular schema. The researcher interviewed the parents/main caregivers, and took notes about the parents' perceptions of schema development.

The parents

They were asked to keep a *record of schemas* they spotted in their child at home. In addition, they were given a chart on which to note any events when schema patterns occurred. (Only one parent actively recorded schemas. This initiative to exchange information about children's learning between settings pre-dated Learning Story assessments for documenting learning using narrative records (Carr 2001), now commonly used in New Zealand.)

At the end of the field research, the action researcher collated all available data, by child, using a coding system based on the schemas located and described by Athey in the Froebel Nursery Project.

Types of data

The three types of data collected about children in the main Competent Children project were also collected about the children in the action research component:

- *Data about the children* 15 time-interval observations (five at three sessions); assessments of some competencies gathered in the month prior to her fifth birthday, and parent and key workers' perceptions of other competencies exhibited by children at the same age.

- *Data about the centres*   a profile supplied by the head teacher, as well as researcher-rated centre quality using an earlier version of the centre quality rating scale also administered by the Wilton Playcentre in 2003 (see Appendix D in van Wijk *et al.* 2006).
- *Data about the families*   demographic, use of early childhood services, and family life experiences gathered in an interview with the main caregiver.

The Competent Children action research centres

Two centres were chosen for the action research. Their pseudonyms are Elder-tree and Oak-tree centres. These, and the two centres chosen as comparison centres (Matai-tree and Rimu-tree), were purposively selected. Some minimum criteria for inclusion were set:

- at least five children were in the age scope of the main study – that is aged 4–5 – and would be at the centre for six months;
- the parents of the children knew enough English or Samoan to understand what the research was about from the bilingual pamphlets, so they could give their informed consent;
- at least two staff had diploma qualifications in early childhood care and education, and two had at least two years of experience in early education;
- the staff group was stable.

Both the schema and the comparison groups chosen included one all-day childcare centre and one kindergarten sessional group. None were implementing *Te Whāriki*, the New Zealand curriculum for early childhood education, as the draft was just out in 1993.

The staff in the four centres said the competencies expected of their children by the age of 5 were: communication, social skills, early literacy, early mathematics, logical reasoning/puzzles, physical ability, physical dexterity and music.

The children

The selection criterion for the children was that they were aged between 4 years 3 months and 5 years, giving them at least six months' formal early education prior to starting school. The centres' rolls were used to draw a random list of five children who fitted these criteria.

	Schema centres		Comparison centres	
	Elder-tree	Oak-tree	Matai-tree	Rimu-tree
Ownership/ Management	Non-profit; cooperative management	Regional kindergarten association	Non-profit; cooperative management	Regional kindergarten association
Roll	40 over 2s	45 over 3s in mornings (research group)	29 (10 under 2s and 17 over 2s)	38 over 2s in the research group; 3 sessions per week
Family background	Middle class	Lower middle class. Nearly half Māori	Middle class	Lower income; multicultural
Staff	5 full time; 1 part time Half EC teacher qualified and half studying for a EC qualification	3 full time All with EC teacher qualifications	6 full time; 2 part time Three with EC teacher qualifications, three still studying Two advanced	3 full time All with EC teacher qualifications, and head also had a degree
Planning	Whole staff did overall plan. Key workers planned for individuals in 'their' group	Whole staff did the plan for curriculum areas, plus plans for individuals' interests	Whole staff, based on nine basic activities	Whole staff did a plan for curriculum areas, plus plans for individuals' interests on a roster basis
Non-contact time	Minimal non-contact	Non-contact twice per week	Some non-contact	Non-contact twice per week

Figure 1.5 Centre descriptions.

Initially, 12 girls and 8 boys were randomly selected from those eligible. However, the parents of one child did not consent; one left the centre before the data collection was complete; and a third seldom attended and was not included in the analyses. Of the 17 children who did participate, half were described as European-English, 6 as Māori, and 3 were immigrants from Samoa.

Thirty per cent of the schema children and 43 per cent of the comparison children were from average or below-average income households; two households in both groups were high income earners; and the balance were a little above average.

Comparing the schema and comparison children

Checks were made to see whether the children in the schema centres were markedly different from the children in the comparison centres. Few differences emerged although there could be some influence from the comparison children's mothers' higher educational qualifications.

Differences

The educational qualifications of mothers of comparison children were higher, but more mothers of schema children were in professional or semi-professional jobs; the opposite was true of the fathers. Comparison children were described as having a wider range of numeracy skills.

Similarities

There were a number of similarities between the schema and comparison children. For instance, a large majority of the children were read to with a similar frequency (mostly once a day), could write or pretend to write lists, counted out loud and recounted their ages, could recognize their own name in print; a similar high proportion from both groups could write their own name.

Similar numbers in both groups had experienced similar types of changes in their lives (for example moved house, changed household composition, had an absent parent). All had English as their main language, with about 20 per cent of both groups knowing some phrases in another language. In both groups the family income of between 85–90 per cent was derived from wages or salaries, and about 50 per cent had home computers.

The Wilton Playcentre centre of innovation project ■

Wilton Playcentre was designated by the New Zealand Ministry of Education as a centre of innovation for 2003–2006. Its particular innovation was, and is, schema learning and teaching.

Wilton Playcentre

The Wilton Playcentre is a parent cooperative centre, with a full early childhood education licence from the Ministry of Education. It is a member of the Wellington Playcentre Association that is affiliated to a national movement in which parents and children play and learn together. Throughout New Zealand, Playcentre parents are provided with additional learning opportunities to become better educators in centres and at home. Parent educators plan, organize and supervise Playcentre sessions. To equip themselves for these responsibilities, they attend courses and seminars focused on how children learn and how adults can assist that learning.

The Wellington Association philosophy regards the Playcentre as:

A family concept that recognises that children can fulfil their potential most successfully when their parents/caregivers understand and participate in the learning processes. We believe that parents/caregivers are the first and best educators of their children (Wellington Playcentre Association leaflet, *Welcome to Playcentre*).

In 2003, 20 children from 14 families were enrolled at the Wilton Playcentre. The Playcentre offered four half-day sessions each week, but only a handful of families came to all four sessions. At the Playcentre, the same team of parent educators are responsible for the same session each week. The minimum commitments for each family are to undertake the duties pertaining to 'their' session each week, and to attend a meeting once a term to discuss running sessions and children's progress. Attending monthly 'business' meetings and Playcentre Course 1 training are also required.

Data collected from a survey of parents showed that most families wanted to attend Playcentre until their children went to school at around the age of 5. Over half the parents were in paid employment, and the majority of these worked part time in professional occupations that reflected their high academic qualifications (Mitchell *et al.* 2004).

There was extensive involvement in training, with nearly half of the respondents studying for a qualification. The majority of those enrolled in courses were taking Playcentre courses. Others attended Playcentre workshops solely out of interest to understand more about practice in Playcentre settings.

Te Whāriki (Ministry of Education 1996) is the curriculum framework used and it underpins planning and evaluation (see Chapter 2). Child-initiated play, exploring and experimenting dominate, with children having time to complete activities to their satisfaction. Children from a wide age range attend each session, so there is an emphasis on younger children watching and learning from older children, and older children practising nurturing and leadership skills.

Introducing schema theory to Wilton Playcentre participants

Pam Cubey introduced schema theory to the Wilton Playcentre in 1998 during their professional development sessions. She felt that schemas would be a tangible content for developing an emergent curriculum based on children's interests and fascinations. Research in books on schemas by Chris Athey, Anne Meade and Pam Cubey, Cathy Nutbrown and Tina Bruce was shared. For example, she quoted Anne Meade's Lego metaphor to describe what probably happens in the brain: 'Schemas are pieces of thought, which fit in many places, unlike pieces of a jigsaw puzzle. They are more like pieces of Lego, because they can be clustered in different ways to form concepts' (Meade 1996: 1).

The Wilton Playcentre members developed their own descriptions of schemas and responses:

> From time to time, we observe some children who seem like butterflies flitting from one activity to another. If you look closely they could be investigating the same schema using different materials, e.g., putting play-dough in a closed container and then in the oven, wrapping a present at the collage table, crawling inside a crawl tunnel and then falling asleep in a barrel swing, could be investigating an enclosing schema.
>
> (Mitchell *et al.* 2004: 32)

Schemas as repeated behaviour that signify patterns of thought made a lot of sense to Wilton Playcentre parent-educators. [We]

Photo 1.2 Inside a crawl tent.

knew [our] own children seldom liked to repeat exact content – they like variety, yet they have fascinations. . . . [We] could see [our] children through different lenses when [we] understood that a schema fascination indicated exploration of more abstract thoughts such as verticality, connection, transporting, or rotation.

(Wilton Playcentre *et al.* 2005: 51)

The professional development workshops on schemas were run by Pam Cubey at Playcentre until 2004 when experienced Wilton parent-educators took over that responsibility themselves. It was at that time that Harper (2004) developed a schema chart for workshop facilitators and participants (see Figure 1.6).

Wilton Playcentre's centre of innovation research

Like all New Zealand early childhood education centres of innovation, the Wilton parent educators became practitioner-researchers and the Ministry of Education paid for experienced researchers to mentor practitioner-researchers involved in the research project. Pam Cubey was one of the research associates contracted to mentor Wilton Playcentre members.

The Playcentre's action research aimed to increase parent-educator awareness of schemas in their own, and other, centre/s. The researchers investigated:

- the use of Learning Stories (Carr 2001), and schema learning theory;
- the role of documentation in maintaining continuity and quality across sessions, and continuity between Playcentre and home;
- parent engagement and sustaining a Playcentre community of learners.

The overall research project involved five cycles of action research. The action research cycles were:

- early literacy schematic interests and pedagogy;
- the social aspects of schema actions at home and Playcentre;
- continuity and progressions in some individual children's schemas;
- assessment, planning and evaluation based on schemas;
- sustaining a community of learners.

(van Wijk *et al.* 2006)

If a child is passionately interested in items in this column...	They may well be exploring this schema...	And so they might want to use these areas of play in the following ways...							And here are some problems you may have
		Blocks, Puzzles Manipulatives	**Storytelling/ Pretend Play**	**Carpentry Junk, Collage**	**Paint Finger-paint**	**Physically, Active, Music and Movement**	**Playdough, Clay Cooking**	**Sand, Water**	
Picking things up, moving them, and putting them down or dumping them. Perhaps using pram, bag, basket, truck or wheelbarrow. Usually has full hands	**Transporting**	Train set, vehicles, moving the materials in vehicles, sometimes dumping instead of unloading	Shopping with loaded bag or trolley. Journeys, moving house, wheelbarrows, bags, pockets, suitcases, pushchairs, picnics, large shoes on feet	Moving items from e.g. shelves to table. Pulleys, building sites with wheelbarrows and tool aprons. (safety issue: transporting tools)	Work may portray transporting. Carrying paint pots in carrier	Moving things, self or others in wheelbarrows, prams, trolleys. Carrying things, moving big things. Helping get equipment out. Wheels on the bus	Moving playdough from place to place in toy kitchen or to somewhere else in the centre	Wheelbarrows, moving sand. Buckets, containers and jugs for moving water, watering plants around the place	Lost objects. Moving things to inappropriate areas – need places to take stuff to (e.g. sand, water, paint, finger-paint, tools). Picking up yucky things in order to move them. Dumping
Materials that change shape, colour, consistency. Nothing stays clean	**Transforming**	Inventing different ways of using the materials	Dressing up, taking on roles of animals or imaginary characters, wearing masks and wigs, face painting	Gluing, sticking, painting constructions	Paint and colour mixing. Painting self. Painting dye over wax crayon. Papier mâché	Pretending to be e.g. animals by changing gait, posture etc. Window cleaning, washing down messy play tables	Making dough. Clay hardening. Most cooking involves transformation	Wetting, freezing and melting. Adding colours to water, sand and water to each other, smoothing and raking sand. Making froth and bubbles	Mucky messes and other adults disapproving of you allowing such mucky messes, changing clothes frequently

(Continued overleaf)

If a child is passionately interested in items in this column . . .	They may well be exploring this schema . . .	And so they might want to use these areas of play in the following ways . . .							And here are some problems you may have
		Blocks, Puzzles Manipulatives	Storytelling/ Pretend Play	Carpentry Junk, Collage	Paint Finger-paint	Physically Active, Music and Movement	Playdough, Clay Cooking	Sand, Water	
Horizontal, vertical and diagonal movement of things and of self. Things fly through the air, child moves at a run	Trajectory	Building and knocking down. Mobilo ladders. Marble runs, garage ramps, angled planks. Pushing cars off tables	Fire engines with hose and ladders, rockets, spaceships, submarines, window cleaning, aeroplanes, building site, cash register drawers	Sawing, banging, hammering, and tearing	Flicking paintbrushes, throwing painty sponges, painting on easels and floor. Energetic finger-painting. Work may include vertical, horizontal, or diagonal lines	Climbing, slides, swings, trolleys, throwing, kicking balls, stepping up and down, lying flat, rolling, ramps, sloping walls, trikes, waterslide	Rolling pin, banging, hammering, poking, chopping, mashing, pouring, sprinkling	Knocking sand castles down digging, ramps, slides. Squirting, pouring, sprinkling, ladling, tubes, sink or float, pipe systems, hoses popular	Inappropriate biffing e.g. hard objects, things that splat, dinner. Vigorously swooshing a prepared activity off a table
Things that turn, loves wheels and/or balls. Exploring curved lines, loves circles	Rotation and Circularity	Cogs, wheeled vehicles, helicopters, screw tops, winding and unwinding, turning keys in locks. Train track in a circle	Pretending to be or be in washing machines and dryers	Taps, screw tops, wheels, cogs, drills, screwdrivers	Moving hands in circles in fingerpaint, rollers, rolling painty balls. Making spirals, circles, faces	Whirling, tops, dancing, hoops, Ring-a-ring-a-rosy. Turning a parachute. Moving in circles, windmill arms, riding trolleys and trikes in circles	Rolling out. Pastry wheels, mixing, stirring, whisking, a blender. Egg beaters	Water wheels, wheeled vehicles. Cement mixers	Turning dials (heaters, clock hands, stereo volume, toaster knobs)

Enclosure and Enveloping	Surrounds things. Likes getting inside a defined area e.g. a block building, tyre or barrel. Gets into boxes. Covers completely, wraps up. Hides. Gets into boxes and closes lids	Wooden blocks make enclosures for self or objects; houses, cages etc. Animals in fields, doll's house, Lego boundary wall on base plate, Russian dolls, inset jigsaws, posting boxes	Dressing up in face-paint, layers of clothes, bags, and hats. Hiding in caves, beds for dolls and self. Getting under piles of clothes, blankets or cushions. Pretend parcels, pregnancies, buried treasure	Toys in boxes. Wrapping paper around objects. Layers of collage. Papier mâché	Frames pictures, covers painting completely with paint, covers name up. Paint on self, toys, walls. Face-paint	Dressing up, tents, huts, tunnels, barrel swing, parachutes	Playdough in or over toys. Wrapping clay round stones, making clay caves. Peas in pod, eggs, onion, samosas, icing, spreading, buttering. Food in packets	Filling containers, including pliable ones e.g. balloons. Tea sets. Burying things, holes, dump trucks, cement mixers. Volcanoes	Lost and hidden objects. Taking bags everywhere. Wearing too many layers
Connecting	Joining things together. Ties things up	Train tracks, engines and trucks, Mobilo, Meccano, Lego, jigsaw puzzles	Human train, holding hands, tying people up with dramatic play rationale	Gluing, sewing, sticky tape, staples, string etc. ties things up. Paper chains, beading	Connecting patches of colour. Using lines to connect parts of the picture	Ring-a-ring-a-rosy, follow the leader, conga lines, Dem Bones	Gathering dough into bigger lumps. Joining bits of clay with toothpicks	Connecting hose to tap, joining tubes or pipes to make a watercourse	Ties things up, trip wires, knots, shoelaces
Disconnecting	Opposite: takes things to pieces and/or scatters the parts	Building and knocking down towers. Spreading out Duplo, Lego, Mobilo	Undressing: undoing shoes, unbuttoning, unzipping	Cutting up. Tearing. Taking old appliances to pieces		Spreading or scattering things	Cutting playdough and clay. Pulling mandarins to pieces. Rubbing butter into flour	Smashing ice, sandcastles	Emptying out tidied collections. Taking working appliances to pieces

Figure 1.6 Schemas in areas of play.

All five action research cycles yielded information about schema learning. However, in this book, we mainly draw on the first three action research cycles. The relevant research question was: *In what ways does understanding of schemas enable parents to support, extend and enrich children's learning at home and in the playcentre?*

At the time the research began, Wilton Playcentre parents were used to identifying their child's schema interests because of the centre tradition of schema 'spotting' and enrichment.

As Playcentre parent-educators are the children's parents, there is a 'double hit' when they identify, reflect on, plan for and talk about the children's schemas. Discussions at meetings, and observations of actions during the sessions, stimulate reflection on their child's schemes of action and those of any other children at home, as well as their children's friends who come into their home on play dates.

The approach taken

The research approach taken was similar to the Wilton Playcentre's cooperative approach to providing early childhood education. The action research was 'participatory and involved collaborative critique, with most members having involvement in gathering data, examining and critically discussing it, and planning and acting' (van Wijk *et al.* 2006: vii). Parent volunteers took on these tasks, depending on their circumstances, skills and wishes.

Data collection

Like the Competent Children action research, a considerable amount of the data came in formats that were already being used for teaching purposes in the Wilton Playcentre: Learning and Teaching Stories (Podmore *et al.* 2000), observations, photographs and samples of children's work. This documentation, and discussions around that documentation, added another layer of schema awareness. In other words, the nourishment via documentation reinforced patterns of thought and created a double loop of learning. In addition, interviews, group discussions and parent reflections recorded in notebooks were gathered in to find out the views of the parent educators.

Unlike the Competent Children project, there was no data collected relating to children's performance. Instead, throughout the Wilton Playcentre project, the focus was on children's learning progressions and what contributes to them.

Extension of the Wilton Playcentre research

To complete this book, Pam Cubey conducted some follow-up research, compiling six case studies of children's schemas, based on representations of their thinking from Playcentre pedagogical documentation, from family photos and parent reflections in notebooks. From time to time, centre of innovation research writing is used to supplement these sources (van Wijk *et al*. 2006; and an unpublished report by Bulman *et al*. 2005).

A cross-section of children was chosen as our case studies; all were from middle-class homes. Their parents had maintained comprehensive records covering their child's schema interests, some schema extension experiences, and the child's learning progressions. The children were aged between 2 and 5 at the time when their case studies were written. All had attended Playcentre from an early age and regarded it as a second home.

These six case studies found that the parents continued to talk with their children at home and in the community about their schemas and on related topics, and supported their child's endeavours to represent their schemas well into their first year at school. Some detailed findings are presented in Chapter 5.

Plan of the book

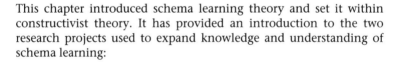

This chapter introduced schema learning theory and set it within constructivist theory. It has provided an introduction to the two research projects used to expand knowledge and understanding of schema learning:

- the Competent Children action research project; and
- the Wilton Playcentre centre of innovation project, and our extension to that research.

Chapter 2 provides the context for the research projects:

- an overview of the policy context, and the curriculum approach in New Zealand that supports schema learning and teaching, drawing some comparisons with the *Early Years Foundation Stage* in England;
- research literature about children's thinking, in particular research about extending children's thinking about schemas.

Chapter 3 reports on the case studies of schema learning from the Competent Children action research project. Chapter 4 presents quantitative outcomes data for the children involved in the Competent Children action research, and moves on to describe some outcomes for the Wilton Playcentre children using qualitative data.

Chapter 5 puts the spotlight on six case study children at the Wilton Playcentre, and explores how their fascination with particular schemas and how schema thinking contributes to early literacy development.

The final chapter draws the threads together and further develops theoretical understandings. It considers the role of teachers in enhancing schema learning and extending children's thinking. Some reflective questions are included for readers to discuss with colleagues.

2

CURRICULUM AND PEDAGOGY: CONNECTING TO YOUNG CHILDREN'S THINKING

This chapter provides the context for the two schema learning projects: the policy context, including the New Zealand early childhood education curriculum (drawing some comparisons with the *Early Years Foundation Stage* framework in England), as well as the context provided by the research literature about schema learning, and about learning and teaching more generally.

Policy goals to improve the quality of early education

If society is to support any government's investment in early childhood education, then the educators need to be able to describe what and how children learn and how teachers facilitate that learning, so that the community can understand the specialized way teachers deepen young children's learning. New Zealand was one of the first countries to develop an early childhood curriculum: a draft of *Te Whāriki* was first released by the government in 1993 setting out curriculum aims, pedagogical principles, and learning goals for infants, toddlers and young children. Its final version was released by the Ministry of Education in 1996.

Specialist training for implementing any early childhood curriculum is important. In 2002, the New Zealand government made a further bold strategic move requiring the large majority of early educators to be qualified, registered teachers by 2010 (Ministry of Education 2002). Playcentre educators are exempt from teacher registration requirements because of the high level of parental involvement in training and running the programmes for their own children and the Playcentre-to-home transfer (similar to 'home educational provision' described by Siraj-Blatchford and Sylva 2004: 726). Play-centre parent educators must have at least minimum training levels in order to maintain a Ministry of Education licence and funding.

Early childhood curricula ■

The early childhood education curricula in New Zealand and England differ in aims and content, and start from different educational philosophic bases. Educational philosophies explain why teachers do what they do. It is useful to know something about the curriculum being implemented in New Zealand where the action research studies were conducted, and the philosophic ideas shaping it. Some comparisons are made with the *Early Years Foundation Stage* framework in England to make the features of the New Zealand curriculum more apparent.

The New Zealand early years curriculum is called *Te Whāriki* (Ministry of Education 1996), a Māori word for weaving. Pedagogical guidance is integrated with this curriculum. It has two broad aims: one related to children's thinking, the term used is 'working theories', and the other to 'dispositions'. The curriculum is used for infants, toddlers and young children in diverse early childhood services (kindergartens, Playcentres, education and care services, home-based settings and *kōhanga reo*, which are Māori language immersion settings) until they start school between the ages of 5 and 6. These services all receive government grants in aid.

The curriculum framework in England until recently has been the *Curriculum Guidance for the Foundation Stage* (Qualifications and Curriculum Authority and Department for Education and Employment (QCA and DfEE 2000)), which had a focus on the process towards and the achievement of early learning goals. It is used by practitioners working with children aged 3 to the end of reception in schools with nursery and reception classes and in early years settings in receipt of Nursery Education funding. Guidance about appropriate and effective practice for children in their first three years, *Birth to Three Matters*, was published by the DfES in 2003. It is described as a framework and it is qualitatively different from the *Curriculum Guidance for the Foundation Stage* as it is 'not encumbered by government requirement or targets or anticipated achievement' (Nutbrown [1994] 2006: 115).

The *Early Years Foundation Stage* (Department for Children, Schools and Families 2007) is a framework that becomes law in September 2008, integrating the *Curriculum Guidance for the Foundation Stage* and *Birth to Three Matters*. This curriculum has four overarching principled themes and 16 'commitments', including working in partnership with parents and the introduction of a key person for every child; it retains the early learning goals for the end of the *Early Years Foundation Stage*.

Te Whāriki: Early Childhood Curriculum

Te Whāriki, Early Childhood Curriculum demonstrates an interactionist stance. As well as drawing heavily on Māori knowledge, the developers were informed by Urie Bronfenbrenner and Lev Vygotsky's social-constructivist theories that emphasize the importance of social contexts for learning. This emphasis is necessary for a bicultural, bilingual curriculum[1] that is implemented in diverse cultural contexts within New Zealand.

The *Whāriki* curriculum provides a framework. The framework is general enough to accommodate a range of philosophies connected to interactionism. Each early childhood setting in New Zealand, including Montessori and Steiner settings, is expected to develop its own emphases that reflect its philosophy, and that are appropriate for the social and cultural background of the families in the community. Nevertheless, the curriculum says that in all settings the learning outcomes should be:

knowledge, skills and attitudes combined together:

- to shape dispositions or 'habits of mind';
- to form the child's 'working theories' about themselves and about people, places, and things in their lives.

Dispositions provide a framework for developing working theories and expertise about a range of topics, activities and materials that children and adults in early childhood service engage with.

(Ministry of Education 1996: 45)

The expectation that knowledge, skills and attitudes will be 'combined together' is different from expectations overseas that children will learn discrete items of subject knowledge, and/or skills.

The strands of *Te Whāriki* are well-being, belonging, contribution, communication and exploration, each with three or four goals such as: 'Children experience an environment where they learn strategies for active exploration, thinking, and reasoning' (Ministry of Education 1996: 16).

The contexts in which children develop are recognized as influencing their learning, as are the relationships between the settings in which young children live and learn – usually their home and an early education setting (Bronfenbrenner 1979). Contexts are recognized in the four principles that complete the curriculum framework:

- the early childhood curriculum empowers the child to learn and grow;
- the early childhood curriculum reflects the holistic way children learn and grow;
- the wider world of family and community is an integral part of the early childhood curriculum;
- children learn through responsive and reciprocal relationships with people, places and things.

(Ministry of Education 1996: 14)

The curriculum introduces responsibility and an ethic of care (contribution) as one of the end-points to early education. Diverse learning pathways are valued. More recently, socio-cultural theory has become evident in the writing and resources for New Zealand educators, in particular the perspective of Barbara Rogoff. In 2003, she said that:

Cognitive development consists of individuals changing their ways of understanding, perceiving, noticing, thinking, remembering, classifying, reflecting, problem setting and solving, planning, and so on – in shared endeavors with other people building on cultural practices and traditions of the communities.

(Rogoff 2003: 237)

In New Zealand, shared endeavours, cultural processes and relationships are strongly emphasized. There is less attention to the first half of her proposition, the part to do with cognitive development. Yet, her point is the importance of shared cultural practices *for* mental processes. We believe that cognitive development has been lost sight of by many educators who just zero in on shared endeavours. The exceptions include practitioners who work with schema theory, who think about children's thinking.

Assessment is regarded as a powerful force *for* learning in New Zealand. Increasingly, children's learning is documented in portfolios or profile books, using both text and photos. Children have ready access to their portfolio to revisit their learning. The four principles of *Te Whāriki* frame assessment in the early years in exemplar resources being produced to assist teachers to assess learning in early childhood settings (Ministry of Education 2004). The authors of the exemplar resources point to possible lines of direction for future diverse learning pathways, and note that socio-cultural approaches to assessment:

- include the children's viewpoint when possible;
- take account of the powerful influence of assessments on children's sense of themselves as learners;
- ensure that assessments of children's learning within a Māori context are situated within a Māori pedagogical framework;
- recognize that assessment is one of the features of a learning community; it influences the quality of children's engagement in learning.

(Ministry of Education 2004: 2)

To date, practitioners using the assessment approach taken in New Zealand often do not show cognitive advances – many are documenting discrete learning events and not showing children's shifts and changes in understanding concepts. The advantages of socio-cultural assessment include being more collaborative, and assisting identity formation: 'the language of assessment and evaluation is one of the routes by which the identity of young persons is formed . . .' (Gipps 2002: 80).

Early Years Foundation Stage, England

The new *Early Years Foundation Stage* in England has some features similar to *Te Whāriki*. The aspirations in *Te Whāriki* talk about children becoming 'confident and competent learners and communicators'. The *Framework* for children from birth to 5 years identifies four principled themes:

- a unique child;
- positive relationships;
- enabling environments;
- development and learning.

The *Birth to Three Matters* framework has been integrated into the new *Early Years Foundation Stage* (Department for Children, Schools and Families 2007), which reaffirms the holistic nature of learning and development, and relationships and interactions with people. It retains the section on schemas.

This integrated curriculum framework is also informed by interactionism. In the 16 commitments, there are features of a traditional school curriculum despite the framework being removed from the *National Curriculum* for schools. The *Early Years Foundation Stage* retains the six areas of learning from the *Curriculum Guidance for the Foundation Stage* (Qualifications and Curriculum Authority, and Department for Education and Employment 2000), but applies these to children from birth to 5 years:

- personal, social and emotional development;
- communication, language and literacy;
- problem-solving, reasoning and literacy;
- knowledge and understanding of the world;
- physical development;
- creative development.

The language in the *Early Years Foundation Stage*, such as children are to 'achieve, or exceed, by the end of the foundation stage' indicates a transmission-of-knowledge view of learning. We have identified a mix of end-points. Some are mastery goals in relation to subject knowledge; for example 'hear and say initial and final sounds in words and short vowel sounds within words', and 'count reliably up to 10 everyday objects'. Most are enquiry processes, including many cognitive development processes:

- *look closely at similarities, differences, patterns and change* [classifying];
- *select the tools and techniques they need to shape, assemble and join materials they are using* [planning];
- *use mathematical ideas and methods to solve practical problems* [problem solving].

(Department for Children, Schools and Families 2007: Statutory Section, 2.14)

Along with formative assessment, there is a statutory assessment system in England, the *Foundation Stage Profile*, which entails summative assessment. Schools must report each child's score against each of 13 scales to their Local Education Authority by the end of the reception year (The Standards Site, DfES, March 2005). In our view, this system could encourage approaches that emphasize the transmission of items of information.

The *Early Years Foundation Stage* and the *Foundation Stage Profile* assessment systems pay minimal attention to the contexts, although the curriculum pays more attention to this through the 16 commitments placed under the four overarching principled themes than was evident in the *Curriculum Guidance for the Foundation Stage* (2000).

The New Zealand system, on the other hand, reflects holistic development, where knowledge, skill and attitudes 'in combination' are fostered to shape dispositions and to promote theorizing about people, places and things. Obviously, theorizing by children is about their everyday lives. Contexts matter in this approach to curriculum.

In both countries, play dominates the pedagogical approaches at least until the age of 5 years, and settings provide a rich array of equipment and materials. Both curricula for 5-year-olds include literacy and mathematics.

How children learn to think

Nuthall (2007: 23) says that teaching (and learning) is 'about creating changes in the minds of students – in what students know and believe and how they think'.

He asserted that effective teaching goes beyond teacher *and* child motivation and involvement (see also Siraj-Blatchford and Sylva 2004). Both are necessary, but not sufficient. Nuthall uncovered, through very detailed observations of students in schools, other elements of learning that effective teachers address:

- students learn what they do . . . the activities students engage in when they encounter content become inextricably bound up in their minds with the content;
- social relationships determine learning . . . long-term successful teaching [in schools] involves working with the peer culture;
- effective activities are built around big questions.

(Nuthall 2007: 36–7)

Nuthall was writing about older children, but the relevance of his first two points for younger children is supported by constructivist research in early education.

His attention to 'big questions' is similar to those who emphasize 'worthwhile' activities. Lilian Katz (1994) frequently stresses the importance of 'worthwhile'; Athey does too: 'Education is a process of bringing up children that develops their knowledge and understanding in depth and breadth in worthwhile directions ([1990]; 2007: 15)'.

The National Academies in the USA helped identify 'big questions' for early education (Bowman *et al.* 2000: 10). These authors provided a synthesis of research focused on early learning that, *inter alia*, identified several foundational 'big' concepts that are the basis of much later learning:

- what is *representation*? (key for early literacy development);
- *quantity* to do with size, capacity, distance, and movement (key in early mathematics);
- *causation* in science.

Athey adds *functional dependency* in science (see Chapter 6 of Athey [1990] 2007).

We would add:

- *position* (topology), and comparison of *patterns* – in relation to mathematics;
- *identity* – in relation to socio-cultural learning;
- *social justice* – also in relation to socio-cultural learning.

While education involves the social world, learning occurs in an individual child's mind. According to Osborne (1985: 82) 'Learners must themselves actively *construct*, or *generate*, meaning from sensory input; for example, sights, sounds, smells and so on. No one can do it for them.'

Vygotsky called this level of development 'micro-genetic development', summarized by Rogoff as 'the moment-to-moment learning of individuals in particular contexts, built on the individual's genetic and cultural-historical background' (2003: 65). Constructivists see these moments as cumulative; the learner encounters a new experience, and holds onto a piece of thought until sufficient other experiences connect with and confirm a pattern and a new concept develops (Nuthall 2007: 71). A new cognitive structure is formed. Rogoff sees 'micro-genetic development' as inseparable from 'cultural-historical development', as history has left a legacy of symbolic and material technologies, as well as values and scripts that learners assimilate or encode in their moment-to-moment learning.

Latterly, most attention has been given to socio-cultural-historical influences on learning. Schema learning reminds teachers and parents of the biological (genetic) aspects of learning.

According to Catherwood and Boulton-Lewis (1993: 23), cognition is an 'interplay' of the processes that are used in all stages of human development. These processes are 'attention', 'encoding', 'representation' and 'memory', with the latter involving the establishment and activation of networks of information or knowledge within the brain or mind. 'Attention', Catherwood and Boulton-Lewis argue, is important for concentrating learners' resources on the most salient information, and 'attentional persistence is likely to be affected by the child's interest in the available task or items' (1993: 27). Children's interest is high when playing. In their earliest months and years attention spans are usually relatively short with plenty of motor activity. 'Encoding' is the ongoing process whereby new data is fitted into patterns already observed (Piaget called this 'assimilation'). 'Representation' in the form of early language usually starts being observable to adults in the later months of the first year of a child's life. Positioning objects to represent forms such as parallel lines is a fascination of toddlers. Other forms of representation, such as painting, develop later in the pre-school years.

Brain development goes from simple to complex or higher order. This matches learning trajectories from basic and concrete to complex and abstract. Significant neurobiological changes need to take place *before* infants and toddlers can do most things – physical and/or mental. The timing of these biological changes is set by genetic programs, then experience – what happens in children's lives – determines the organization of brain cells, the retention and/or strengthening of synaptic links between cells, the chemistry of neurotransmitters, supply of blood, density of 'wrinkles' in the grey matter, and so on. It is not possible to hurry the timing of genetic programming.

The functioning and organization of the brain produced by nature and nurture 'dancing together', and reflecting where each individual has invested great physical and mental activity, are reflected in individual competencies – physical, social and mental.

Competency in thinking is more than a matter of cognitive structures forming, however. Habits of mind – dispositions – play key roles in thinking. In addition to ability, two components related to

Photo 2.1 Lining up parallel objects.

thinking dispositions have been found to be important for good thinking:

- Inclination [or interest]; and
- Sensitivity about appropriateness of actions.

(Tishman 1994: 12)

'Interest' features strongly in New Zealand endeavours related to dispositional learning. Similarly, 'fascination' is a word often used in relation to schemas in young children's thinking – a child's intense interest and repeated actions can help adults identify his or her schematic form/s of thought. Generally, younger children are not sensitive about the appropriateness of their actions, as the story about Rosa and the laptop in Chapter 4 indicates.

In Chapter 1, Nina's mother described how Nina's eyes lit up and she became excited when she spotted a spiral. Such affective engagement helps memory processes. Indeed, brain structures for memory processes and handling emotions are co-located. Their interaction results in memories being imprinted with emotions – they will be implicit memories in the case of schemas and 'inclinations' (dispositions).

As has already been noted, theorists differ in their stance about how much a learner constructs their understandings within and through social environments. The principles in *Te Whāriki* lead most New Zealand early educators to emphasize social environments, but a number of writers are bringing the physical environment and objects and tools back into focus (for example Ramsey *et al.* 2006; van Wijk *et al.* 2006). There is widespread agreement that young children actively construct their understandings about 'people, places and things'.

According to Vygotsky (1978), young children learn by putting together insights from diverse first-hand experiences. Every piece of learning, he says, is based on earlier experiences – and for young children they must be real-life experiences. Piaget (1926) and Bruner (1971) emphasize children's actions with objects in their theories. They noted three broad levels – action, representation and abstract thought – in their theories. This is the framework used by Athey in the Froebel Early Education Project ([1990] 2007).

The forms humans use to represent people, places and things – language, visual art, poetry, music and drama – have an impact on how we think and what we think about: 'If different forms of representation performed identical cognitive functions, then there would be no need to dance, compute, or draw' (Eisner 1997: 349).

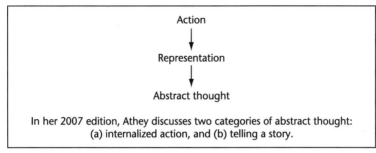

Figure 2.1 Levels of cognitive development.

The contribution of pedagogical approaches

Extension of schema learning matters. Standardized test scores of the Froebel Institute children showed that 'the experimental group made highly significant gains in test scores that were sustained during the first two years of primary education' (Athey [1990: xi] 2007). Those children had their schema experiences enriched both by their teacher and their parents.

Not flitting, but fitting

One of the insights gained from Athey's research was that young children may be paying attention to particular patterns, scientific principles, or even concepts, but the way they pay attention is not observable in the same way as it is in older children or in adults who are learning a concept.

When observing young children in early childhood centres that are using a child-centred approach, adults often think that children are like 'butterflies', flitting from area to area, from child to child. That may be true some of the time. However, when integrated learning is taking place, another metaphor might be more appropriate: that of 'bees' that gather nectar to integrate it into something of significance. Children focus their attention by fitting new experiences into patterns they have already stored in their memories. They develop a schema by behaving like honey bees, moving from experience to experience to gather further ingredients to encode; in that way, they build a fuller understanding of that schema. In other words, children get hooked on certain patterns of behaviour because they are trying to make sense of the abstract characteristics of particular features of their environment, such as 'vertical', by fitting them into cognitive structures they already possess.

Athey, Nutbrown and other schema researchers, including ourselves, have all demonstrated that young children show this 'attentional persistence' or 'interest', as they 'encode' new instances of schemas (for example Arnold 2003; Mitchell *et al.* 2004). Nutbrown describes this in terms of obsessions.

The behaviour and the thinking process associated with children being fascinated with particular forms of thought has been described by Meade (for example 1994) as a process of 're-cognition'. 'Re-cognition' involves different kinds of information, from new experiences or insights, being clustered in the child's mind and feeding existing cognitive structures. 'Encoding' (fitting in information) and 'representation' (forming a cognitive impression of the information) are the terms Catherwood and Boulton-Lewis (1993: 23) use to describe the same process. 'Memory' is also drawn on to build more sophisticated cognitive structures.

In order to cluster different kinds of information, children need a variety of information sources. According to Brierley (1987: 111), 'The brain thrives on variety and stimulation. Monotony of surroundings, toys that only do one thing, a classroom display kept up for too long, are soon disregarded by the brain.'

Play entails variety, involvement and fun. 'Children who do not play are not exercising their clusters of schemas' (Bruce 2005: 90). Intellectual development and feelings work together in brain development. As Bruce points out, 'All forms of play appear essential for the intellectual, imaginative and emotional development of the child and may well be necessary steps to a further stage of development' (ibid).

A nourishing environment

Athey and Nutbrown's research projects confirm that two principal observable ways younger children 'come to know' are via their *symbolic representations* and their *active exploration*. In order to explore in these ways, children need an environment that feels safe and predictable.

Effective educational provision for young children must have consistent features which can be considered in terms of three 'constants':

– adults and their behaviour,
– routines and information,
– experiences and materials.
... These three 'constants' – adults and their behaviour;

routines and information; experiences and materials – help to create a consistency of curriculum which enables children to be *active* and *independent* learners who:

- tackle new things because they feel safe in doing so, because they are stimulated to try and because they know that adults will help if needed;
- plan what they will do when they arrive – for example deciding 'When I get to nursery this afternoon I'm going to paint some wood and fix it together' or 'I think I might make a den this morning';
- revisit familiar materials to build on previous experiences such as returning to the brick area to build again a structure which was fun to make yesterday or adding new things to a drawing or more details to a story.

Knowing that adults, space, time and materials will be 'constant', the same today as yesterday, helps young children to assume more responsibility for what they do and to follow their consistent threads of thinking and doing without unnecessary hindrance or over-dependence on adults.

(Nutbrown [1994] 2006: 27–9)

Time to play is very important. It is central to young children's learning. But play is not the only means through which they learn. They learn from imitating role models, and by joining in everyday experiences at home and in the community. Nutbrown ([1994] 2006: 119) believes that 'Children must also have opportunities to experience the new and the challenging as "apprentices" to adults who can help to extend their thinking and doing'.

Children helping with everyday chores use their action schemas in different ways.

The role of adults

Athey (2007), Nutbrown (2006) and Bruce (2005) all endorse the importance of the social mediation of learning. Teacher attention and parent involvement are significant in helping children extend their schematic patterns of thinking and construct mathematical, scientific and literacy concepts. Their experiences accumulate. This is more likely where there is continuity in adults' pedagogical practices between home and the early education setting, 'a parent–teacher partnership' (Athey's book sub-title).

The EPPE project team in England report that good outcomes were found when information and regular feedback about progress was given to parents that supported the parents to engage in complementary educational activities in the home (Siraj-Blatchford *et al.* 2003: 146–7). It should be noted that the EPPE authors said this applied regardless of the theoretical approach used.

A good deal of adult attention goes on identification of schema interests in settings where teachers use schema learning theory. But effective education entails more than identification.

Nutbrown (2006) asks, 'What do you do when you think you have identified a child's schema?' Her answer is:

> It is not sufficient simply to identify a child's interest: early education needs to challenge children's thinking and extend their learning. When a child appears to be paying attention to a particular pattern, he or she needs to be provided with a range of interesting and stimulating experiences which extend thinking along that particular path.... Extensions to children's schemas need to provide opportunities for further learning, for children to talk and for more nourishment for children's fertile minds.
>
> (Nutbrown [1994] 2006)

The importance of talking

As well as opening up experiences and adding equipment, opportunities for children to talk need to be extended. Athey ([1990: 111] 2007) cites studies showing that children work longer and produce work on a higher development level when they talk about their experiences with adults. Recent research confirms that 'teacher questioning, dialogue, story and play are central to the process of developing ... young children's thinking' (Ridley 2007: 13). Language – such as adults or older children naming schemas and actions, engaging in conversations that relate to young children's form of thought (and content connected to those schemas), and asking challenging questions – is necessary for extending thinking.

Nutbrown ([1994] 2006) believes that variety and stimulation must be complemented by the 'important experiences of talking with adults'. Children need to be able to ask questions in order to make sense of the world, and they deserve answers which do just that – make sense. She is critical of flippant or autocratic closed answers:

> To reply to a child's why question with an answer such as 'because it is' or even 'because I say so!' will not suffice because such responses are neither logical nor satisfactory in terms of their thinking, and do not do justice to children's capacity to

think through what they encounter as they try to make sense of
what they find.

(Nutbrown [1994] 2006: 8)

There is another important reason for children to talk with adults
about their experiences as they happen. Often young children do not
know the words that go with their explorations. If a child first hears
the word 'grid' in the context of discussing her own paintings, it is
likely to be far more effective than if she comes across it by herself in
later childhood. If she has not heard the word 'grid', then she will not
say it. If she has neither heard it nor said it, how will she get on in
middle childhood when she comes to read it? How will she further her
emerging knowledge of geometry if she lacks the relevant vocabulary?

Obviously, it is important that teachers are well informed so that
their talk is of high quality: if young children are exploring 'tessellation' as one of their space-order schemas – and they do – then teachers
need to know about tessellation themselves.

Schemas – the core of developing minds

Jean Piaget (1962) states that: 'Schemas of actions [are] co-ordinated
systems of movements and perceptions, which constitute any elem-
entary behaviour capable of being repeated and applied to new situations, e.g., *grasping, moving or shaking* an object'. Athey ([1990] 2007)
endorses Piaget's view that schemas are cognitive structures that can
be 'organic', 'static' or 'dynamic'.

Nutbrown (2006) used the term 'threads of thinking' for her book
title, and described schematic patterns in children's play and language
and in their thinking.

Schema learning

Children can and do express their interest in a particular schema,
such as 'circular dynamic' in many media – dance, visual art, music
language, and so on – calling on a range of cognitive processes, albeit
focused on a particular schema or clusters of schemas. Tina Bruce sees
'a child's schemas are a resource, an access mechanism, which can be
used to tackle any area of knowledge' (2005: 92).

Athey ([1990: vi] 2007) wanted to find out more about the develop-
ments of *symbolic representation* and in the *abstract thinking* of individual children, and how early childhood programmes contributed
to young children's forms of thought, commonly known as schemas.

Like other constructivist schema researchers, ourselves included, Athey found that young children's representations are dominated by symbols (visual arts and mark-making connected to emergent written literacy), with fewer records of representation through drama and music.

After two years of field work at the Froebel Institute, which involved collecting and analysing over 5000 observations of what young children do, Athey found that:

- children are fascinated with patterns (schemas), some of which stem from their perceptions of the world, and some of which stem from actions;
- 'thoughts' develop as children internalize and cluster schemas;
- adults working with children's schemas bring marked and lasting benefits for children.

Symbolic representation

Athey uncovered the fascination young children have with particular patterns. Some of the patterns are *figurative schemas*, exploring the 'look' of objects in the natural world and artefacts in the man-made world, and/or spatial order, such as 'grids'. Some schemas stem from and are about actions, such as 'going over and under' (*action schemas*).

There is often no clear-cut distinction between figurative schemas in drawings, paintings and models made by young children, and action schemas. Children may be dealing with both the static and dynamic aspects of an idea; for example a circle and a spinning wheel simultaneously. Athey found *figurative* and/or *action* patterns represented in children's drawings, 'writing' (called mark-making) and language, and, therefore, in their thinking. Athey categorized symbolic representations into three subdivisions.

Athey ([1990] 2007: 53) also states that:

> Different writers refer to these three forms of representation by different names. Bruner (1974) describes the three modes of representation as 'enactive', 'iconic' and 'symbolic speech'. Piaget differentiates between 'operational', which has its basis in action, and 'figurative', which is based on perception. He refers to speech as a system of signs.

Abstract thinking

In terms of children's development of thinking, Athey confirmed that for each type of schema there is a sequential progression. For action

1. *Graphic* representations of the *static* states of objects
   (configurational or ikonic)

'Tree'

2. *Action* representations of the *dynamic* aspect
   of objects and events

'Sawing'

3. *Speech* representations of either static or dynamic aspects of the
   objects or events that accompanied representations of 1 and 2:

   'Walnuts fall off the tree, . . . so do leaves.'

Figure 2.2 Graphic, action and speech representations.

schemas the three-stage sequence is motor behaviour, symbolic representation and abstract thought. From her observations, she discovered that prior to the abstract-thought level children spend time exploring 'functional dependency relationships'.

In early education, 'functional dependency relationships' can be seen when 'children observe the effects of actions on objects or material' (Athey [1990] 2007: 70). For example, Brenda (at 4 years 7 months) was observed dancing around a maypole holding one of the ribbons, and reversing the direction of her dance from time to time. Brenda told a teacher excitedly, 'When I go round the string gets shorter', and demonstrated the truth of her observation. Then she danced in the opposite direction and shouted, 'It gets longer' (Athey [1990] 2007: 140).

Athey also found that:

[I]n everyday cognitive functioning, particularly as children become more mature and acquire more experience, 'thought' reflects clusters of schemas that contain a wide range of content. In brief, schemas become co-ordinated with each other and develop into systems of thought.

(Athey [1990] 2007)

An example of a connection between early schemas and later coordinated concepts is the 'back and forth' schema seen in a toddler who brings items and dumps them in the lap of a familiar adult. These may become coordinated (or 'connected') later with 'going and coming' between home and the early childhood centre. Added together, these two periods of exploring the 'transporting' schema may form the foundation of map-reading that is developed in middle childhood.

In the 2007 edition of her book, Athey devotes a chapter to 'Continuities between Schemas and Concepts'. Her examples illustrate how clusters of schemas learned in early education used by children in primary school classes are efficient ways to solve problems of measurement (shortest railway route between towns, length of a work-bench in pencil units), force and economic geography (consequences of traffic jams), to name but a few.

Photo 2.2 Block construction exploring space order.

Figural representation which stems from perception

Chris Athey ([1990] 2007: 61–3) included children's drawings, paintings and three-dimensional constructions in *figural or static representation* linked to early perception.

Athey found that the marks made by children were generally lines, curves and space orders – and that space orders were 'drawn' twice as often as either lines or curves.

Lines

When exploring lines, children between the ages of 2 and 5 started with vertical scribbles and progressed through 13 other schemas to drawing two right angles. Of these, the children were most likely to draw or paint vertical lines or a picture containing grids (see Figure 2.3).

Curves

When exploring curves, the children started with circular scribbles and worked on a total of 10 schemas, finishing with multiple loops. The most frequent representations were the circular scribble, then a circular enclosure or core and radial. The understanding that a 4-year-old must have developed in order to distinguish between a helix and a plane spiral make it clear that work with these schemas is hard intellectual work. Athey found that usual progression is as shown in Figure 2.4.

Space order

In space-order schemas, children start by exploring proximity between marks or objects and progress through to representing 'in front of' or 'behind' and, finally, the same figure in different positions. Athey's observations showed that the space-order schemas are systematically related to increases in age. The usual progression is as shown in Figure 2.5.

When working on space-order schemas, children begin to think about the following, very complex abstract concepts (usually in this order):

- proximity;
- enclosure;
- connection;
- separation;
- horizontal and vertical coordinates.

---

1   vertical scribble (the effects of vertical action of the hand)

2   horizontal scribble

3   continuous horizontal and vertical scribble

4   horizontal and vertical differentiated scribble

5   open-continuous triangle (the zigzag)

6   horizontal line

7   vertical line

8   straight parallel lines

9   grid

10   stripes

11   triangle

12   rectangle

13   right angle

14   two right angles

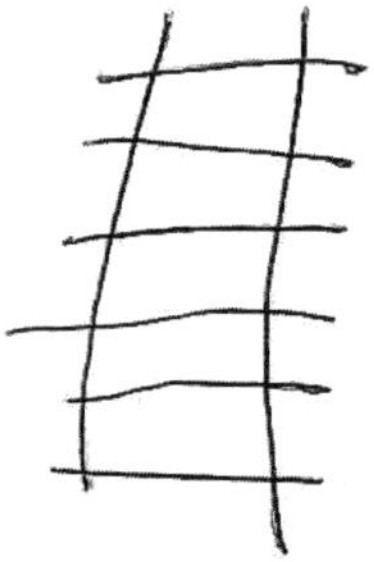

'A ladder'
('grid')

(Athey [1990: 79]; 2007: 62)

In the second edition, Athey brings some of these together under a heading called 'Angles, Triangles and Quadrilaterals'.

Figure 2.3 'A ladder' ('grid') which coordinates many line schemas.

When working with marks or building with blocks, young children often intend not only to represent real-life objects – which is what adults expect when they ask, 'What is it?' – but also to explore a different form of thought: schemas. If children show a heightened consciousness of certain content in the environment and repeatedly draw and paint these objects, it is logical to conclude that they are drawing or painting in order to explore the schemas implicit in the objects – and that these schemas/forms are the ones that are dominating their thinking. Adults thinking about children's thinking are able to cue into both possibilities.

Early childhood educators who have studied the curriculum offered in early childhood centres in Reggio Emilia, Italy will recognize the

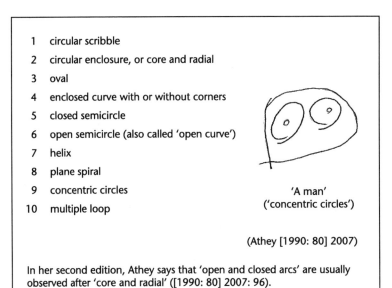

1   circular scribble

2   circular enclosure, or core and radial

3   oval

4   enclosed curve with or without corners

5   closed semicircle

6   open semicircle (also called 'open curve')

7   helix

8   plane spiral

9   concentric circles

10   multiple loop

'A man'
('concentric circles')

(Athey [1990: 80] 2007)

In her second edition, Athey says that 'open and closed arcs' are usually observed after 'core and radial' ([1990: 80] 2007: 96).

Figure 2.4 Curves.

way the Italian teachers nourish these forms of thought in young children. Once any forms of thought (schemas) are identified, teachers can plan curriculum extensions and enrichment. Given an abundant supply of materials and experiences, the children will also extend the curriculum themselves.

Dynamic representation which stems from action

Athey identified eight categories of *action schemas*:

		Occurrences
1	dynamic vertical	403
2	dynamic back and forth, or side to side	357
3	dynamic circular and rotation	280
4	going over, under or on top	204
5	going around a boundary	133
6	enveloping and containing	351
7	going through a boundary	259
8	'thought'	163

(Athey [1990: 130] 2007: 115–16)

1   proximity between marks

2   vertical order of elements within figure

3   horizontal order of elements within figure

4   grid order within figure or within enclosure

5   grid order inside and outside discrete figure

6   proximity between figures but no order

7   vertical order between figures

8   horizontal order between figures

9   grid order between figures

10   representing 'in front of' and 'behind'

11   representing figures in different positions

'A house by the river.'

(Athey [1990: 80] 2007: 63)

In the 2007 edition, Athey labels 10 and 11 as 'projective space' schemas.

Figure 2.5 Space order.

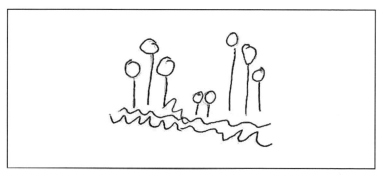

Figure 2.6 Space order – proximity and separation.

Athey found that when advancing in their development of action schemas, the Froebel Institute children progressed from 'motor' behaviour through 'symbolic representation' to later 'conceptual' thinking. 'The largest number of motor-level examples occurred at 3 years 1 month; symbolic representation at 4 years 1 month; and thought level at 4 years 5 months' (Athey [1990: 69] 2007).

In other words, behaviour associated with each of the action schema showed continuity and progression. Motor-level examples of particular schema in individual children came before symbolic representations of these schemas, and later still, coordinations of schemas at the thought level. In her discussion of 'vertical dynamic', for example, Athey ([1990] 2007) describes an incident where Amanda was exploring the effect of weight changes on her ability to lift things up ('functional dependency relationship').

> Amanda (3 years 6 months) put water into a balloon. She told the teacher that the balloon filled with water was heavy. Mrs B asked how she knew. Amanda said, demonstrating, 'Look, I can't lift it. I can lift this.' (lifting the one filled with air).
>
> (Athey [1990: 133] 2007)

Seven months later, Amanda was thinking about the 'vertical dynamic' schema and the concept of 'down' entirely in the abstract.

> Amanda (4 years 1 month) 'You know leaves? They fall off the tree on to the ground [pause] and acorns fall off the tree'.
>
> (Abbey [1990: 133] 2007)

Alistair's development of an understanding of 'circular direction and rotation' was cited in Chapter 1. He was described at each level: first 'motor level', then 'symbolic representation', then 'functional dependency relationship' and, finally, 'thought level'. These four levels followed each other as Alistair grew older. First, he tried 'rotation', then talked about it as he tried it; later, he experimented with it and, finally, he could think about rotation in the abstract.

Nutbrown ([1994] 2006: 34) describes how teaching actions connected to schemas facilitates learning:

> Children's schemas, identified and nurtured, can provide opportunities for continuity in learning. Children's persistent threads of action and thought seem to be fundamental elements which link what children do and think with process of learning and with its content. This kind of continuity where children create their own continuities in the process of exploring, thinking and learning, belongs at the heart of any discussion of curriculum continuity. Viewed in this way, schemas can be considered the core of children's developing minds.

Planned learning ■

Planned learning occurs when teachers bring theory and practice together to shape the way they guide learners. The teacher must know enough about individual children to orchestrate activities or processes that could 'take children a stage further forward from where they were' (Moyles 1989: 15), and to influence their cognitive development by changing their understanding (Rogoff 2003: 237). Knowing which schemas fascinate children helps teachers and parents connect in order to discuss and plan interesting and appropriate learning experiences together.

Johnston (2005: 176) says, 'Planning and preparation are essential prerequisites for effective teaching and learning. [Yet] In many ways the plans are less important than the process of planning'. All early educators know that young children take planned activities along exciting new pathways, if given the opportunity. This is why the PLOD (*Possible* Lines of Direction Concept (Bartholomew and Bruce 1993: 48) has had enthusiastic take up. Discussion of a PLOD plan means that teaching teams can have appropriate resources on offer and be mentally prepared for scaffolding children in order to advance their thinking. (For take up in New Zealand, see Ministry of Education assessment exemplars, 2004). Poplur (2004) talks about such planning enabling teachers to be 'poised to give opportunities for exploration and extensions to the children's thinking' (p. 89).

Effective planned learning for young children mean the curriculum should not be compartmentalized into subjects. As Nutbrown ([1994] 2006: 3) reminds us:

> Young children cannot be taught effectively if planned learning is always artificially divided into man-made compartments called subjects. . . . Children will explore scientific ideas, learn about mathematics and develop their language while engaged in many different experiences in home and community situations as well as through experiences specifically planned for such learning in early childhood settings.

The two research projects reported in this book used schema theory to inform the researchers', teachers' and parents' observations of children at play and participating in home learning environments. They wanted to learn more about how children think, and about their 'working theories'.

Both studies reported in this book have been influenced by Athey's findings about children thinking about mathematical and science-related schemas ([1990] 2007). Her focus on form has flowed into our research. The New Zealand projects entailed researchers working with educators and parents. The adults in both projects used schema theory in their practice. And they used other theory too. Doing research was intellectually challenging for the adults. The scores from the Competent Children sub-study indicate that the adults' mental work flowed through into the children's mental work (cognition) with positive effects. The case studies of the Wilton Playcentre children indicate that educators' practice informed by schema theory fostered diverse learning progressions.

Note

1 New Zealand has two official languages: English and Māori.

SCHEMA DEVELOPMENT IN NINE CHILDREN

■

Chapter 3 describes the schema action research component of the Competent Children study: its approach and what those undertaking the work found out in relation to interactions, social competencies in children, communication skills, dispositions, early literacy and early numeracy.

The Competent Children action research study ■

Cathy Nutbrown continued the work of Chris Athey in Britain, bringing the perspective of an early childhood teacher and adviser to her research. Her book is 'an attempt to think more deeply about children's actions and interactions and is a voyage of discovery into the riches of children's minds' ([1994] 2006: xiv).

For the New Zealand Competent Children sub-study, the teachers in the 'schema' centres learned more about schema theory and its application, and their experiences threw light on how early childhood teachers can think more about children's thinking. As the Competent Children project is primarily an outcomes study, its action research was designed to help explain *any differences in results* between the schema children and the comparison children, rather than to advance the theory developed by Athey.

Multiple observations

It can be challenging to 'schema spot' in centres with many children and lots happening. Different observational techniques were used in the Competent Children action research so that the schemas could be confirmed when various sets of observations were read in conjunction with one another.

Parents reported anecdotes. Teachers did too, in a more systematic and recorded way, keeping some records in the form of schema charts. One researcher visited each centre once a month and carried out running records through a half-day period; teachers also included something similar in the assessment portfolio records they kept of the children. Another researcher visited centres on at least three half-days to collect time-interval observation data, using an observation schedule containing pre-coded categories (see Appendix on p. 159).

The multiplicity of observations – and observers – was useful in identifying the schemas with which the children were absorbed during the six-month research period. For example, if the teacher keeping anecdotal records was unsure whether a pattern of action was being repeated, often it could be confirmed by the action researcher's running-record observations of the child or in the other researcher's time-interval observational records.

Case studies of schema children

These case studies of the schema children show periods of absorption with *figurative schemas* (static representations of the way children perceive the world) and/or *action schemas* (based on actions). As many of the children worked on both types of schema, some feature in both sections of the chapter. Paul's work on figurative schemas was so interwoven with his action schemas that all his data is given together in one section. (The names used are not the children's real names.)

Bob lines, space orders

According to his mother, Bob had been focusing on 'lines' and both the 'vertical' and 'horizontal order' between objects off and on for over a year, and exhibited this pattern of behaviour at the centre as well as at home. She said that he placed toy cars neatly in line ('horizontal order') and balanced his skateboards on top of each other ('vertical order'). Her mention of more than one skateboard also signified his interest in 'dynamic horizontal', a possible action schema extension of his lines schema.

The teachers also felt that Bob was working on the 'spatial order of lines' and on 'dynamic horizontal'. When he was aged 4 years

Figurative	Action
Lines	Dynamic lines
Curves	Dynamic circular
Space orders	Going over, under, through, enveloping, containing

Figure 3.1 Types of schema.

8 months they pasted into his portfolio (home book) a painting covered with blue, orange, and some black, vertical, and horizontal lines. The action researcher discovered more examples of Bob working on figurative schemas to do with horizontal and vertical lines, or space order.

> Bob (4 years 7 months), with two boys, was loading small vehicles on the flat roof of a toy garage. Bob told the boys where to park them until all the garage area is full ('proximity' and 'horizontal order between items').

Bob took about 30 minutes to make two caterpillars by painting egg cartons and lining up those he had painted on the floor ('horizontal order between items or lines'; see Figure 3.2).

> Bob (4 years 8 months) was painting egg cartons with cotton buds and pallet paints, with a friend. Bob lined up the finished product on the floor in a careful neat arrangement. He had been working there for 20 minutes already. He drew on a carton with a pencil before he painted it. Again, he aligned the finished carton with the others, precisely. He took one back to the table. 'I need a tail on it, I've got two caterpillars.' [After a conversation with his friend] Bob returned to painting another carton, different colours down each side. He went to look at what the girls were doing three times; then returned to his work. He had lined up 10 cartons. . . . He took one back and painted its 'feet' carefully and thoroughly with yellow, then said, 'I am going outside now.'

The time-interval observations of Bob confirm patterns of behaviour related to 'lines', 'dynamic horizontal' and 'dynamic vertical': 10 of the 15 one-minute observations included mentions of these schemas. Examples from observation notes include:

> Bob (4 years 8 months) stood painting at an easel. . . . He drew flowing

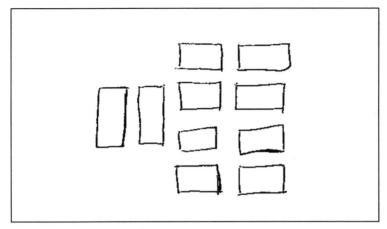

Figure 3.2 Bob's line-up of cartons.

long lines ('stripes') and large circles ('curves'). [Later] Bob walked to the art table. He got some scissors and some wool. He cut off pieces of wool ('lines').

Emma horizontal lines, vertical lines

Emma's mother thought that she was working on several schemas, but felt that 'enveloping' was dominant. The researcher's notes confirmed both points. The paintings in her home book indicated that Emma was interested in a series of vertical patterns. The researcher provided a running-record observation of Emma (4 years 8 months) at the easel near a teacher:

> The teacher asked her whether she would like to do another painting. Emma said, 'Yes.' The teacher suggested, 'You could do a pattern like the picture you have just finished, where you went up and down, up and down, and go right across the page.' Emma replied, 'I went like this,' demonstrating vertical lines with her finger. She began to paint the picture. The teacher reflected Emma's actions in words. 'You're using white paint, red paint, and white paint again. The shapes look like triangles. Your brush is going up and down, up, up.' Emma laughed.

(This was one of the rare occasions when a researcher observed a teacher providing language support for a child working on a schema.

Photo 3.1 Figural representation schema.

According to the researcher's field notes, this teacher reflected children's schemas with appropriate language increasingly.)

The second observation captured Emma exploring 'dynamic vertical' while also using the 'static grid' of ladders.

> Emma (4 years 8 months) was outside. She climbed the ladder on to the cable reel, talked to a boy, then climbed down the ladder and straightened the mat. She climbed the ladder, jumped across the space between the cable reels ('dynamic horizontal') and climbed down. She repeated this four times ('dynamic vertical').

Probably, Emma was also exploring some functional dependency calculations coordinating what she had learned about momentum and connection.

Jan and *Sam* connecting

Jan and Sam attended the same centre. Jan's mother was very quick to appreciate schema development when the theory and the dominant schemas were described to her, and she immediately gave several examples of Jan's 'connecting' schema:

Jan (4 years 9 months) tied all the laces from shoes between or to chairs all over the house.

Jan (4 years 10 months) was very interested in a TV programme on trains and asked how they were all stuck together. Soon after he joined cushions together on the floor and joined pegs together in long chains.

Jan (4 years 10 months) arranged video cassettes on the floor all in a row, touching.

Several weeks later, prior to Jan starting school, she reported that he seemed to have lost interest in this schema, and no other schemas were dominating his behaviour.

The staff and action researcher had difficulty in identifying any repeated pattern of exploration, and little showed up in the time-interval observation records, except that once Jan was seen on the obstacle course walking across the planks and ladders that 'connected' the 'separate' boxes and cable reels. Two undated pieces of artwork in Jan's art portfolio demonstrate an interest in 'connection'.

Sam's mother also responded immediately with descriptions of his obsession with connecting through space. She said that he was 'into tying chairs together'. Although much of Sam's behaviour was challenging, it was noted that he was able to stay on-task for quite a length of time when absorbed with 'connection' schema behaviours. Like Jan, he spent time in and around planks which 'connect' boxes, and on making 'connected' trains.

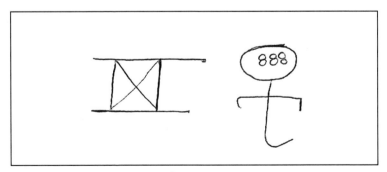

Figure 3.3 Jan's art ('connection').

> Sam (4 years 11 months) was sitting on the sofa watching four children balancing and walking across a plank balanced across two boxes like a bridge ('topological space', 'connection'). A parent helper was standing in the doorway talking to the children on the plank. She then turned and walked away. Sam jumped off the sofa and jumped across the plank in front of one of the boys. The boy said, 'Hey; I'm walking.' Sam looked at him and smiled. He lay underneath the plank and tried to lift it as the boys walked over it. One of the boys said, 'I'll tread on you.' Sam laughed and carried on pushing his arms up to try and lift the plank ('functional dependency', 'going over', 'connection').

Sam's attempt to lift the plank while the children were on it gave him functional dependency information that a connection may be made stronger when there is a weight factor.

On two days, about a week apart, Sam was observed pulling trains around a room:

> Sam (4 years 11 months) was sitting on a mat with another boy with the Duplo blocks and trains. He had a train with four carriages behind, pulling it along the mat going 'Ummm, ummm, ummm.' Sam pulled it behind the boy who sat and watched him. He pushed it hard into a pile of bricks and it broke up. Sam said, 'Oh, no' ('connection', then 'separation').

> Sam (4 years 11 months) had seven little carriages ('connection'), part of a train set. He pushed this around the floor and headed into another room ('dynamic horizontal').

Later that day, a teacher helped Sam make physical connections by fixing his rod and line. A few minutes later, when he asked her how to make a fish, she used language to do with tying ('connection'), demonstrating that she understood that Sam would want to join the 'fish' to the line.

> Sam (4 years 11 months) was pretending to catch a fish. His fishing rod fell apart ('separation') and the teacher fixed it [without using any 'connection' language]. Sam took his rod and line to another area and pretended to catch' ('connect with') a fish.

Half an hour later, Sam was in the tree fort with another child. They had fishing rods made of sticks and wool with a block of wood (his 'fish') tied to the end of the wool.

The teachers recorded Sam at a younger age exploring 'connection' mechanisms:

> Sam (4 years 7 months) carried some rope outside with Raymond. They

linked two trolleys together with the rope. The rope fell off so there was some joint problem-solving as to how to attach ('connect') the rope to the trolleys. In the end, Sam sat on the back of one of the trolleys holding the rope link to the other.

Figurative and action schemas, interwoven

A number of children explored the static and the dynamic variations of schemas at the same time. One child provided striking examples of this pattern.

Paul circular enclosure, core and radial, dynamic circular

Paul was the youngest of the schema children. He appeared to be working with several schemas, and was the only child who could provide a case study of 'circular enclosure', 'core and radial' and 'dynamic circular'. Paul's data is presented together because there seemed to be a close link (within minutes sometimes) between him working on 'circular enclosure' (a figurative schema) and 'dynamic circular' (an action schema).

Paul was observed using 'circular enclosure' in 5 of the 15 observation periods. He chose the sandpit encircled by a tyre in preference to the oblong-shaped sandpit. Paul (4 years 8 months) spent over five minutes one morning examining two rolls of Sellotape™. At the end of that week, he combined his interests in 'circular enclosure' and 'connecting'. With a considerable amount of time and effort, he tied a cord around one wrist, enclosing it. Then, with help from an adult, he tied the other end of the cord around his other wrist (another 'circular enclosure') 'connecting' one part of his body to another: a powerful learning experience about the state of connectedness.

Another day, Paul (4 years 10 months) walked around with a cardboard tube and tried to fit it over a variety of items or fit things into it ('circular enclosure').

> Paul (4 years 4 months) followed [supervisor], helping to tidy the centre. He kept moving his hand in and out of a towelling elastic hair ring ('circular enclosure'). He found a wheel ('circle') and gave it to [supervisor].

> Paul (4 years 5 months) moved to the sand trough in the other room, poured sand on to the water wheel ('core and radials' and 'dynamic circular'). He had the wheel turning well. [Another child] put a handful of sand on the wheel. Paul said, 'No, don't help me.' He stopped it

Photo 3.2 Paul fitting things into a cardboard tube.

turning, got the container for pouring and refilled it. The wheel became clogged, so he put his finger in and unblocked it ('dynamic circular', 'functional dependency').

By immediately identifying the source of the blockage, Paul demonstrated his understanding of the function of the 'core' of the wheel. The inner rod had a circular enclosure to which the radials were fitted; sand or water poured on those radials caused the wheel to turn as long as the inner circles were not restrained by friction.

At the age of 4 years 7 months, Paul was observed twirling a lasso ('dynamic circular'). Later, on the same day:

Paul made a crown at the collage table and placed it over two yoghurt cartons joined together ('circular enclosure'). After taping strips of card to larger card, he moved into another room and twirled his lasso ('dynamic circular'). [Ten minutes later] Paul 'juggled' a ball ('dynamic circular'), then tied a scarf around his head ('circular enclosure') and lay down and 'slept'.

Nearly an hour later, when the researcher returned to observing Paul, he was working with his lasso.

Paul was attempting to lasso a tree. He threw it around the tree several times, rotating it before throwing it ('dynamic circular', 'functional dependency'). He threw it on top of the fort, then on to the veranda railing.

In his work with this trajectory schema – an action schema where an object moves through space – Paul had observed, through his own actions or from TV, that rotating a lasso before sending it to 'catch' another object helped its speed and/or distance. This coordination of schemas was still fascinating him a month later:

Paul (4 years 8 months) was swinging a rope around, attempting to throw it over the branch of a tree ('dynamic circular', 'trajectory').

Later that day, the action researcher became involved in another of his experiments with the 'dynamic circular' schema.

Paul took a length of wood and returned to the outside playground. He tied the rope to the wood and I helped secure it to a tree. He swung back and forth, then side to side, then round and round ('dynamic circular'). I used words to describe his movements to him.

When Paul was aged 4 years 7 months, his parents completed some observational records. On the first day he drew 'a painting with circular shapes – said it was a "fire hose".' A day later, Paul had built a 'pin-wheel special machine out of a shoebox, with pins [forming] a circular protrusion out the side and stuck out the top' ('circular').

The teachers' anecdotal observations also contained many examples of Paul's fascination with 'circles' and with 'dynamic circular'. One of Paul's paintings, at age 4 years 5 months, used a 'circle and radials' (see Figure 3.4).

About the same time, the staff noted that Paul had spent some time 'holding a cape in his right hand, whipping it around and around'. At age 4 years 8 months, the head teacher wrote in Paul's portfolio (home book), 'He has a fascination with things that go around – spirals and pieces of string that he can twirl around' ('circular dynamic'). Aware of his fascination (as well as with 'connection'), the staff provided Paul with materials – rope, sewing tape, string – to

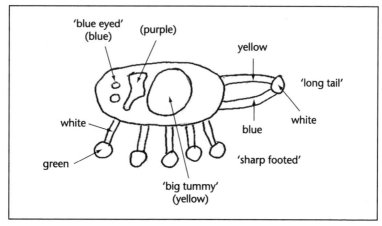

Figure 3.4 Paul's 'smiling funny creature' ('enclosures', 'radials').

Figure 3.5 Paul's Dad paintings – approximately one month apart.

facilitate his learning around these schemas. They also took sketches of his art, noting the repeated patterns or figurative schemas of 'circular enclosure' and 'core and radials', as well as 'grid order outside of a discrete figure' (see Figure 3.5).

During the last interview before he turned five, Paul's mother described his ongoing interest in 'circles and radials', and commented that he makes things 'using bottle tops to "turn things on" such as radios' ('dynamic circular', 'functional dependency').

These schema explorations were an enduring pattern over months. There are no records of Paul at thought level with the action schema associated with 'circles', possibly because adults concentrated on concrete actions and drawings in their observation notes, and because Paul seldom had contact with adults at the centre (he talked to a teacher only twice in 15 time-interval observations – when he got sand in his eye, and at snack time). Although there are no records of any abstract conversations, Paul's rapid solution to the problem of sand clogging the water wheel suggests that he had reached the thought level.

Action schemas

Action schemas are described as operational systems of knowledge by Athey ([1990] 2007: 114). She points out that they involve more conceptual thought than figurative knowledge.

Bob dynamic vertical, dynamic horizontal

Some of the things Bob was doing with 'vertical' and 'horizontal' in his figurative work were described earlier, and it was noted that he was also interested in the dynamic forms of these schemas. He had two skateboards, which allowed him to make comparisons relating to differences in size, weight and wheel qualities; in other words, exploration of functional dependency relationships. The following examples suggest that Bob was at the functional dependency stage – or thought level – in his work with 'dynamic horizontal' schemas.

In the first example, Bob was working with and thinking about 'dynamic vertical' and exploring the higher-order concept of height:

> Bob (4 years 8 months) was sitting on a see-saw in the garden, in the middle holding on. One other child was on the end. Both were laughing and rocking. The other child said, 'Let's do it high, eh?' Bob smiled, moved off the see-saw and got back on at the other end, knelt, and said, 'Yes, really high' ('vertical dynamic'). Both began to rock and chant together, 'Waay, waay, waay.'

Bob was demonstrating this thinking that he could be higher if he knelt on the end, rather than sitting on the see-saw ('functional dependency relationship'). He saw parts of his own body as units of measurement. He used the operation of addition – his upper legs added to his body – to gain height.

In the next example, Bob coordinated a 'dynamic horizontal' action with 'straight parallel lines' schema to solve the problem created by his taking a 'dynamic oblique line' with the truck.

> Bob (4 years 9 months) pulled a truck towards a tree ('dynamic horizontal') and tried to fit the truck through the gap between the sandpit and the tree. It got stuck so he pushed it back, lined it up ('functional dependency relationship') and pulled the truck through the gap and smiled.

The researcher noted that Bob smiled when he solved the problem. Most schema researchers have noted indications of positive affect linked to schema actions.

There are lots of schemas being coordinated in the following 'experiment'.

> Bob (4 years 10 months) tied a piece of wool which was attached to a nail in a block of wood on to the tie from his hood. He tried to pull the wood along by walking backwards but the block of wood kept turning over on the sandy soil and getting stuck, so he held the wool about 18 inches from the wood and pulled it until he reached the concrete path. He then let go of the wool and walked backwards, letting the hood tie pull both the wool and the block, gradually walking faster as the block slid easily over the concrete.

In this example, Bob figured out that the length of the ties contributed to the difficulty of 'transporting' the wood over the rough horizontal surface. There are indications that he had prior knowledge of the effects of resistance.

Anita dynamic horizontal

Anita's intellectual fascination with 'dynamic horizontal' actions provides examples of the way children explore 'dynamic horizontal' schemas. Her teachers first noted her interest in 'lines'.

> Anita (4 years 5 months) was sitting on the floor with two girls pushing a truck along a track. She helped to rebuild the track, fitting the pieces together competently.

The value of free-form materials is also demonstrated in the following exploration recorded by the researcher a month later.

> Anita (4 years 6 months) was inside. She scooped sand from the trough on to the floor ('dynamic vertical', 'trajectory'). She crawled on the floor, stood and danced, scraping her feet along the sandy floor. She filled a funnel with sand, moved around the room allowing the sand to flow on to the floor. She said, 'Everybody', shuffling rapidly, 'Everybody.' She ran in a circle, shuffling.

About 15 minutes later, she was still experimenting with sand on a horizontal surface:

> Anita vigorously swept the table free of sand with a wide arm movement. She tipped another container of sand on to the cleared table and swept it thoroughly again. She fetched a broom and swept the sand on the floor with a broom, back and forth. Then she got a dust pan and brush and swept the sand with that brush for another five minutes ('dynamic horizontal').

The following week, the researcher noted that Anita spent 15 minutes with another child trying to push a large wooden train up slopes and along paths outside. It was recorded that she often used her own body to explore 'dynamic horizontal' schemas.

> Anita (4 years 9 months) fitted one cardboard carton inside another and walked around with it balanced on her head. . . . Anita (4 years 11 months) was walking around with her feet in beakers.

In both these examples, she was moving objects horizontally by wearing them: she was coordinating 'enveloping' with 'dynamic horizontal', perhaps to explore the functional relationship between weight added to objects and speed of movement.

In the following example, the teachers provided materials that would afford her further tactile experience of 'dynamic horizontal'. Here, the content (finger paint) assisted speed of movement.

> Anita (4 years 11 months) was finger painting – reluctant to begin with, but soon very involved – moving her hands very energetically on the table.

Susan boundaries, going between, maps

Susan's mother reported her intellectual interest in 'maps', and referred to 'boundaries'. Teachers' records confirmed Susan's interest in maps. At age 4 years 2 months, according to the portfolio, 'Susan draws pictures of maps and machines – works with care and concentration.' About the same time, the staff observed:

> She has shown an interest in following the boundary of the centre fence line, and on walks follows lots of different tracks . . . often interweaving.

Small groups going on walks in nearby parkland was a regular routine at the centre Susan attended. The numerous different tracks allowed her to explore traffic routes and the notion of 'going between'. At age 4 years 6 months, Susan was painting maps and tracks (see Figure 3.6).

Susan, Stephanie, Chris and *Emma* containing, enveloping

The teachers and action researcher noted Susan doing quite a lot of wrapping ('enveloping') when she was about 4 years 8 months. She wrapped blocks in tissue as presents for children who were pretending to be asleep in beds ('enveloped') on the floor, and put these under their pillows. She also wrapped all her art up in parcels.

The first example of 'containing' will be very familiar to all who know children of this age:

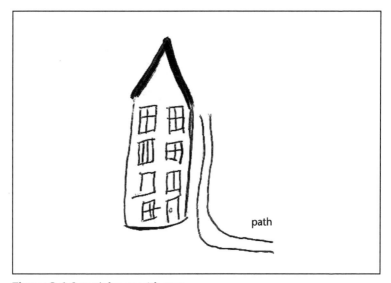

Figure 3.6 Susan's house with map.

Susan (4 years 10 months) spent quite some time filling different containers with sand, first a pot, then an ice-cream container.

On another day, Susan was intellectually fascinated by changes to different objects when they were immersed ('enveloped') in water.

Susan (4 years 11 months) was with two other children by a basin of water. She had a sponge and pushed it in, then pulled it out and squeezed it, twice. [An hour later] Susan was in the shed with another child experimenting with flowers in the basin of water. She selected one, turned it upside down and then pushed it up and down in the water, watching the changes to the petals. 'These are octopuses, eh?'

Stephanie was engaged in an interesting range of explorations. 'She seems to be into everything at the same time,' her mother said. More than most other children in the study she engaged in complex pretend play at the centre, which, by definition, involves drawing on a large range of past experiences and cumulative knowledge. Susan was also frequently involved in these pretend play activities with Stephanie. They shared an absorption in the same schemas and probably enhanced each other's understanding of 'enveloping' and 'containment'. (Given the amount of pretend play, it is likely that these two children were also working on social schemas.)

Stephanie's mother reported her interest in 'enveloping', saying that there was a lot of wrapping things, and putting things into beds and covering them up. This was also observed at the centre by the researcher and teachers. She was fascinated with parcels, wrapped and stuck with Sellotape™.

Stephanie (4 years 6 months) announced, 'We are going on a picnic. That's a nice spot.' She carried two plastic bowls and three chocolates (in reality, blocks) and a container of pipe cleaners to Susan on the couch. They wrapped the blocks in paper ('enveloping') and then hopped around the room, 'We're rabbits.' Stephanie lifted the inverted plastic container and hid the parcels underneath ('enveloping', 'containment'). Three other girls pretended to go to sleep. Stephanie and Susan hopped to them pretending to be Easter Bunnies and hid the parcels under their pillows ('enveloping'). The girls woke up and 'ate' their 'chocolates'. This play was repeated and sustained for 30 minutes.

Ten days later, when the researcher did a running record observation of Stephanie, wrapping ('enveloping') was going on.

Stephanie (4 years 6 months) folded a piece of paper into a parcel and sealed it with six strips of Sellotape™ . . . Stephanie joined two girls in decorating me. Next she found a milk bottle top and covered a bottle with it, taping it on . . . Stephanie made several firmly taped parcels of 'fish and chips' for the 'bird' [another child].

On her next visit, a month later, the researcher was 'enveloped' in decorations by Stephanie, Susan and another girl:

Stephanie (4 years 7 months), Susan and Barbara decided to decorate me as I sat observing them. They made necklaces, decorations, wings, and presents which they draped over me. . . . Stephanie was sitting with another child on a chair. Both were putting fabric on to soft toys and covering them.

Outdoor play also presented opportunities for trying containment.
Stephanie also experimented with 'enveloping' using natural materials.

A group of children were pretending to be a family working in their garden. Stephanie (4 years 8 months) brought pieces of shrub she had broken off, poked a hole in the ground and 'planted' the pieces, patting the soil around the plants ('enveloping' the bottom half).

Photo 3.3 Children contained in a barrel swing.

This action was repeated and lasted for more than 20 minutes.

Stephanie's exploration of floating/sinking an object in water described below (where she started to explore a more complex concept, putting together her understanding of 'enveloping' and other schemas) is an example of an opportunity lost by a teacher. It started with Stephanie engaged in pretend play with Susan and two other children where a small stone was the 'baby' in a 'family' of stones.

> Stephanie (4 years 10 months) said, 'This is the baby stone,' then moved out of fantasy play, and commented that another stone was heavier. She went to a teacher and said, 'Can we get some water to float this one?' The teacher agreed. Stephanie fetched a bowl ('container') and put water in it. She tried to see if the 'baby' stone would float, and found it sunk like the heavier stones ('enveloped/contained'). The teacher did not join the group to provide language which could enhance their thinking.

Stephanie used her own body and senses to explore 'envelopment/containment'. Like many children, she enveloped an object in her mouth.

> Stephanie was having afternoon tea in the kitchen. Rather than eating her plum, she put it into her mouth and felt it, and pushed it out. She repeated this action several times.

One morning when the action researcher carried out running-record observations, Stephanie used containers twice.

> Stephanie (4 years 11 months) and three girls are in the bookshelves playing with dolls. They have 'lollies' in cups. . . . Their 'babies' are in a large green box with a fitted lid. Stephanie puts the box into a larger yellow tub; then takes it out.

Stephanie's portfolio captured some additional explorations of 'containment'. It began with a list of the schema the teachers thought Stephanie was working on at age 4 years 7 months. The list was mostly figurative schemas observed in her many creations. 'Connection' and 'containment/enclosures' (action schemas) were also included. The teachers' commentary continued:

> Stephanie is very interested in copying what she sees. Susan painted a picture of a teapot, then Stephanie painted an almost identical one ('figurative representation of a container'), but she added a handle and a spout.

A teapot in a painting was noted again in a later (undated) entry in her portfolio. The teacher went on to describe other 'containment' behaviours.

> Stephanie has painted another teapot – a 'happy' one with a smiley face and even brown tea coming out of the spout ('trajectory' as well as representing what had been 'enveloped' in the container). She has done a series of 'enveloping' with embellishments: folded paper and card taped as a parcel, with flags and fringes. One is amazing – a flat, decorated, cardboard container which has been decorated with many pieces of work folded and stored inside ('enveloping/containing').

Just as Stephanie and Susan, in their centre, shared an interest in this pair of schemas, so did Chris and Emma in the other centre enrich each other's understanding.

Chris was reported to be aggressive at home, where there had been family problems, but she played quietly at the early childhood centre. The action researcher first noted a pattern of behaviour to do with 'containing', all in one morning.

> Chris (4 years 7 months) was lying in the bottom shelf of the storage cabinet with Emma. They were chatting to each other. . . . Chris is now matching and fitting shapes in a form board ('containing'). . . . Chris tips blocks on to a table and then puts them back into the container.

A month later, her concentrated work was more focused on 'enveloping'.

> Chris (4 years 8 months) stood at the trough. She selected a plastic duck, scooped water and poured it over the duck ('enveloping'). As the duck floated away, she threw water further ('functional dependency'). She retrieved the duck and poured water gently over it. Next she used the duck as a scoop and filled a small container until it overflowed ('enveloping'). She repeated this action several times.

In a series of observations, Emma showed that she was focusing on 'containing/enveloping' in her explorations too. An observational record in her portfolio described her at age 4 years 7 months first using a small bottle to fill a large bottle with water: 'I'm putting some petrol in' ('containment'). She went on to make a cup of tea for Chris ('containment' again), and wrapped up a parcel ('enveloping'). A week later she was described as making and eating a sandwich ('enveloping' twice over), before doing a painting of a big blue patch surrounded by three pink and purple patches and an orange patch.

The action researcher observed a whole sequence of activities to do with 'enclosure or enveloping' in the space of 45 minutes.

Emma (4 years 10 months) was at the creativity table, sellotaping a folded piece of paper ('enveloping'). She then made and fastened a watch strap around her wrist ('enclosure'). Next Emma cut up some straws and put them into a plastic container ('containment'). Emma moved to the painting easel and painted a picture ('enclosures' dominated, although there were other schemas evident).

Emma moved outside and sat in a cart ('containment'). Then got out and with Chris pushed a third child in the cart.

While many of these patterns of actions were to do with capacity – the capacity of various containers, exploration of other aspects of measurement was evident, such as the quantity of paper needed to wrap an object and the length of paper needed to make a 'watch strap'. Both require mathematical thinking about three dimensional objects.

Nutbrown found that three commonly seen schemas had distinct links with mathematical concepts:

- the 'dynamic vertical' schema was evident where some children were involved in activities and ideas concerned with height;
- 'dynamic circular' schema was evident where some children were exploring aspects of rotation and roundness;

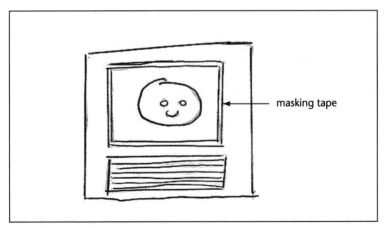

Figure 3.7 Emma's painting – masking tape is used for the frame for the TV picture.

- 'containing/enveloping' schemas were evident where instances of capacity were observed.

(Nutbrown [1994] 2006: 60)

In addition, observations of the 40 children in her study showed that some other mathematical and scientific ideas arose from all three of these schemas, including: 'tessellation; spatial order; surface area; shape; sorting; cause, effect and functional relationships; and colour' (Nutbrown [1994] 2006: 70).

Discussion ■

Communicating with parents

Good communication with parents was important. In initial meetings, parents proved yet again that they are the experts about their own children. It is possible that it was the parents who provided the children with more of the language enrichment to enhance schema development. Teachers were seldom recorded doing this, but were more likely to provide additional materials relevant to children's schemas.

Curriculum materials

Materials enrichment was not onerous for teachers. All children made full use of the wide array of curriculum materials readily available in the two centres to nourish their current schemas. Materials with open-ended possibilities were particularly useful. If the children have to wait passively for adults to provide activities for exploring schemas, or play with a few limited resources put out by adults, they would have far fewer opportunities to experiment with and think about 'vertical' or 'circles' or 'containment', and so on. However, in these play-based, richly resourced environments, the children's powers of inventiveness, visible in their patterns of behaviour, seemed to be boundless.

Excursions

There is a noticeable difference between the New Zealand centres studied, and the Froebel Nursery studied by Chris Athey ([1990] 2007). Athey recorded many occasions when the children went on

Photo 3.4 Imaginative use of diverse materials.

excursions, which served both to trigger new threads of thinking and to nourish several children's schemas. Children in the New Zealand project were taken on fewer excursions, apart from walks in the neighbourhood.

Language enrichment

There was a difference in the amount of language enrichment provided when the New Zealand running records were compared with those provided in Athey's book. Limited conversations between adults and children on any topic whatsoever was a finding that is consistent with other research (for example see Meade 1985). Language interactions were more likely to be about rules and routines, such as putting things back on shelves, sitting while eating, and so on.

One New Zealand teacher did show consistent skill in, and dedication to, reflecting the patterns of children's behaviour (schemas) back to them in the language she used, although she did not have much time with the target children because of the large group size. Most other staff used language related to schemas intermittently.

The researchers checked whether the low level of language enrichment was because the teachers and/or action researcher were leaving language out of their observational records. (This, in itself, would be worrying because it would imply that language was not seen as part of learning experiences worth recording.) However, the records did reflect the language that occurred. When the time-interval observational data was examined, it was found that adult–child conversations occurred during only 8 per cent of the observations – a finding of considerable concern. Providing children with language that helps them represent their thinking was the exception, not the norm.

The qualitative data from the Froebel Institute research (Athey [1990] 2007) gives the impression that there was far more teacher talk with the children, about their art, and about their forms of thought (schemas). At times, it was very explicitly instructional and, it appears, helpful to the children's learning.

> Gary (4 years 2 months) asked the teacher if he could 'read' to her. After they settled he said, 'Look!' and swivelled a pencil. The teacher expressed interest and said, 'You made that turn around didn't you? You made it "*rotate*".' Much later Gary showed the teacher a picture of a concrete mixer in a book. The teacher said, 'That's interesting, you have found something else that goes around, that rotates. Can you think of anything else that "*rotates*"?' After a pause Gary replied, 'Yes, a candy floss maker.'
>
> (Athey [1990]; 2007: 128)

Tina Bruce, the teacher, remembered Gary's interest in the 'dynamic circular' schema and supplied appropriate language to nourish it. More than that, she asked him to use his memory and recall other things that 'rotated'. He did.

What emerged from the New Zealand data was a picture of a higher level of staff reliance on materials enrichment to nourish children's schemas, and a lower level of staff interaction. Note, however, that free access to outdoor materials provided many opportunities for the New Zealand children to explore schemas such as 'enveloping' and 'containment'. This does not excuse teachers' paucity of language enrichment. Socio-cultural theories emphasize the importance of language interactions for children to develop their understanding of the world they live in. With minimal language, how do children consolidate their thoughts about either figurative or action schemas, and progress to understanding concepts? Hopefully, parents are filling this gap (Tizard and Hughes 1984; Worthington and Carruthers 2003).

In the case studies on individual children's schema work, it was clear that Paul and others were developing or had 'working theories' in relation to action schemas. Susan, for example, was developing a 'working theory' or concepts in relation to floating, sinking, and water pressure, and to porous properties, when experimenting with 'enveloping' living and other materials in water. First, she put a sponge into water, pulled it out and squeezed it. Later the same day she was fascinated by the transformation of a flower that she had pushed up and down in another container of water. There was some continuity in content (experimenting with water), but her main continuity was *continuity of thought*.

One example of a child demonstrating a sophisticated 'working theory' was when Paul immediately removed sand that was creating friction in the core of a wheel, thus stopping its rotation. Another example was Bob pulling a block of wood along the ground by two ties and knowing how to adjust the tautness of the ties to cope with different surfaces.

Engaging with children's thinking

But adults did too little to help foster a better understanding of what the children were experiencing, because they did not engage with the children's thinking. For example, when Paul was observed for over a month refining his 'working theory' about 'trajectories' by using a lasso at varying speeds to 'catch' different objects across different distances, no teacher discussed his experiments with him in the researchers' hearing. It was obvious that Paul was capable of abstract thought about science concepts, but the adults did not give him opportunities to talk about his thoughts or test his theories against what adults know about these matters.

In a description of Stephanie experimenting with baking soda and vinegar, there were many comments made by the children as they tried to understand the chemical reaction. However, according to the records, the teacher did not ask many 'Why do you think?' questions to stimulate theory development, nor did she offer much theoretical explanation herself. Many commentators have noted the lack of such discussions in early childhood settings, which they attribute to teachers' feelings of inadequacy in relation to mathematical and scientific knowledge.

Handling curriculum intervention ■

It was a challenge for the teachers to give special attention to the target children. It was noticeable that the one teacher performed much better on language enrichment for the target children. What is more, she taught in the centre with the largest roll (45 in the group). Paradoxically, she accomplished the language enrichment for

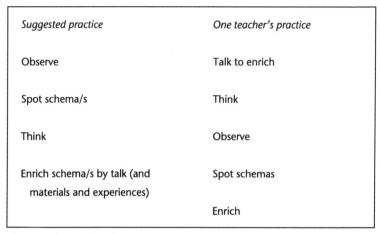

Suggested practice	*One teacher's practice*
Observe	Talk to enrich
Spot schema/s	Think
Think	Observe
Enrich schema/s by talk (and materials and experiences)	Spot schemas
	Enrich

Figure 3.8 Enrichment options.

some by doing it for *all* 45 children. Perhaps this is easier than remembering, 'This is a target child in the research, and I should be providing language to help her schema development.' And it is also possible that, in the process of her thinking more about children's thinking, she was spotting schema interests in far more children and talking about schemas more.

This reflection on the exceptional teacher may also suggest that curriculum intervention could be handled in a different way. For the research, teachers were encouraged to observe and 'spot schemas', then undertake curriculum interventions (including language interactions). Moving straight to language enrichment related to possible action schemas, and reflecting on the children's thinking evident in their talking as it occurs, may be an effective alternative.

4

OUTCOMES FOR CHILDREN FROM SUPPORTED SCHEMA LEARNING

Chapter 4 provides some quantitative findings from the Competent Children action research study, and explains the differences between the schema and comparison centres in terms of social mediation and enriched environments helping children's recognition and recall, thereby fostering cumulative learning. The conditions that supported schema learning found in the Wilton Playcentre project are also explored. The strong coordination between children's homes and Playcentre – because parents are the educators in the early childhood setting – helps to explain the enhanced links between schema and content learning.

Competent Children schema study

The Competent Children research team assessed nine competencies rather than used a single outcome variable such as an IQ score (see Figure 4.1). Like adults, young children have strengths and weaknesses in different areas of their development. 'Individual differences due to genetic and experiential variations and differing cultural and social contexts have strong influences on development' (Bowman *et al.* 2000: 5).

The researchers did not call the competency areas *intelligences* or use the theory of multiple intelligences as propounded by Gardner (1983). There were three main reasons for this. First, the focus of the study was a range of behaviours that demonstrated *competence*. Second, the concept of competence fits the *Te Whāriki* curriculum discourse of 'knowledge, skills and attitudes combined together'. Third, measures of IQ are narrowly conceived and the results are often

Competencies	
Socio-emotional (settled and contributing)	
Communication	Interview with adult
Exploration	
Social problem-solving (interpersonal competency)	
Early literacy	
Early mathematics	assessment of child
Logical reasoning	
Motor skills	
Intrapersonal competency	observation

Figure 4.1 Competent Children project: the nine competencies.

unstable for young children. Instead, a range of competencies were measured by three approaches (see Figure 4.1).

Note that the measure of *early mathematical* competency used for the Competent Children project was predominantly about the recognition of patterns and categories, and a sense of numbers, not their manipulation. The measure used for *intrapersonal* competency targeted young children's complex pretend play.

Competencies

The nine competencies were placed in two categories:

- 'be-ing' competencies;
- 'doing' competencies.

Competencies were categorized for both philosophic and pragmatic reasons. It should be noted that the distinctions are somewhat artificial in that children are 'being' themselves and 'doing' things at the same time.

'Be-ing' competencies

The four 'be-ing' competencies were:

- social-emotional

- communication
- exploration
- intrapersonal.

The first three of these were drawn from the strands in *Te Whāriki*, although a measurement for two curriculum strands ('belonging' and 'contribution') were combined under the heading 'social-emotional' because it proved too hard to find separate research measures for them.

These four competencies are about a child's 'be-ing', rather than about what a child can 'do'. Technical challenges if testing were to occur persuaded the Competent Children research team to tap into the first three competencies by interviewing a significant adult in the preschooler's life, asking for their assessments. First, none of these competencies can be measured by a stranger. Second, using rating scales would have had technical difficulties if the children's mother and teacher had done them without working together to establish shared definitions. Instead, the same interviewer interviewed the parent and teacher to elicit the assessment. (In the pilot study there was strong agreement between their ratings.)

The Competent Children team called the fourth competency 'complex pretend play' (Howes and Gulluzo 1989). It was rated after observing the child in the centre at least three times. Tina Bruce uses the label 'free-flow play', which encompasses pretend play.

> Free flow play enables children to apply what they know, reflect on it, use it in different ways, experiment and explore with what they know and have learnt of relationships, feelings ideas, thought and the movement of their bodies.
>
> (Bruce 2004: 167)

'Doing' competencies

Five competencies in the study were about what the children could do. They were:

- social problem-solving;
- early literacy;
- early mathematics;
- logical reasoning;
- motor skills.

This set of competencies was assessed in the context of an interview with the children about one month before they started school on their fifth birthday. By that time, the child would have seen the interviewer in the centre and at home up to four times.

Some findings from the Competent Children schema study ∎

With a few exceptions, the outcomes were more positive for the children in the schema centres than for those in the comparison centres. These results appear to be associated with the schema children having more interactions with adults and more opportunities for exploring materials.

Social mediation

An analysis of the time-interval observations of the children (see Appendix on page 159) revealed that the most common child-initiated interaction with an adult was a short verbal exchange (one-third); other forms of interaction such as a cuddle, request for help, and a conversation occurred with slightly less frequency. Four per cent of time was spent as an onlooker, observing what others were doing.

For the most part (90 per cent), the adults did not initiate contact. Most adult-initiated child interactions were simple greetings, questions and answers, or comments. At the time, early childhood teachers in New Zealand were influenced by a nativist view of the child – most set up the environment and then observed the children's play.

The dominant social interaction skill of the target children was in the category called 'simple interactive' (45 per cent of observations); whereas only 16 per cent engaged in 'pretend play'. These were at the two ends of a continuum of the Howes and Gulluzo scale (1989).

Some differences were found between the schema and the comparison children. There was more 'pretend play' in the schema centres (19 per cent of the observations, compared with 11 per cent), and schema children were about twice as likely to be engaged in 'parallel play' as their peers in the comparison centres.

In child-initiated adult interactions, schema children were more likely to be engaged in 'conversations' with their teachers (9 per cent compared with 5 per cent) and 'request help' (6 per cent compared with 3 per cent) – factors that would contribute to their better scores. The low percentage of time adults spent in conversations with children is of concern. Research in Britain (for example Whalley 2000; Siraj-Blatchford and Sylva 2004) confirms the importance of adults and children engaging in sustained shared thinking, and of conversations about past and present experiences.

'Complex pretend play', indicating intrapersonal competency, is the final competency associated with cognition. It was observed by the researchers during 7 per cent of the time intervals in schema centres and 4 per cent in comparison centres.

Exploration of materials

Problem-solving was not a common occurrence in all centres, especially verbal problem-solving. 'Exploration with materials' to solve a problem occurred 14 per cent of the time, and was far more prevalent in the schema centres (28 per cent compared with 13 per cent). This verifies the qualitative data analysis that teachers' curriculum innovations in response to children's schemas were dominated by additions of objects.

Cognitive extension

Data indicated that children in the schema centres were spending more time on activities with cognitive extension possibilities; namely, 'experiences that are challenging, but within reach' (Bowman *et al.* 2000: 5).

At times, teachers say they become 'stuck' for appropriate ideas to extend children's experiences and thinking. However, adults in centres using schema learning theory found the opposite. Informed educators and parents buzzed with ideas for additional opportunities for children to be able to repeat their schemes of action.

About outcomes

Results about the three 'be-ing' competencies indicate differences between children attending the schema and comparison centres (see Table 4.1). Because of small cell sizes, tests of significance were not used. The comparisons are the scores to attend to. Differences between competency means are, in part, due to there being variations in the number of sub-scales making up the scores for different competencies. Thus, it is not appropriate to conclude that the schema children were better at communication than social skills.

Table 4.1 Mean scores for children's 'be-ing' competencies by centre type

	Schema centres	Comparison centres
Social emotional		
social skills (peers)	10.05	9.43
social skills (adults)	12.50	11.43
self care	12.40	12.86
Communication		
receptive language	19.75	18.43
expressive language	16.50	14.71
Exploration		
curiosity	16.35	14.00
perseverance	18.95	15.57

Table 4.2 Mean scores for children's 'doing' competencies by centre type

	Schema centres	Comparison centres
Early literacy	16.33	7.86
Early numeracy (student interview, Ministry of Education 1995)	15.20	14.70
Spatial logical reasoning (Raven's coloured matrices)	6.13	4.00

The higher mean scores for children in the schema centres indicate they were perceived to have greater strengths than children in the comparison centres. The range of scores for each variable showed no consistent patterns *vis-à-vis* the schema and comparison children; see the example for Exploration (see Table 4.1).

In the 'doing' competencies, more positive outcomes for children in the schema centres were also found.

Here again, the differences between means for different competencies are, in part, due to there being variations in scoring approaches. It is not appropriate to compare the schema (or comparison) children's early numeracy with their logical reasoning scores.

It would appear that when children's work on schemas is nourished, this assists their literacy skills; for example, they are more likely to understand that mark-making represents other things, they have worked on 'lines' and 'curves', and they appreciate 'connected' versus 'separate' (which is important for identifying what a word is). Parents enthusing about reading and reading books to children are of considerable benefit as well (Snow *et al.* 1998). The Wilton Playcentre research supports this (see Chapter 5).

In summary, with a few exceptions, the Competent Children schema centre scores were better than those of the comparison centres. Greater impact showed up in the data for most of the 'doing' competencies: early literacy was the most marked.

Interpreting the early numeracy data

The data on early numeracy were puzzling in that comparison children's scores were closer to those of schema children. There seem to be three possible explanations. The first is to do with the parents' background of the comparison children, the second with numeracy (and literacy) being fostered in the home, and the third with the instrument chosen to measure early numeracy achievements.

The family background

Generally, children who have mothers with higher education qualifications do better in the education system. More of the comparison children had mothers with higher educational qualifications, yet the schema children scored better. It could be argued that the comparison mother's educational levels may have been influential on one variable, namely, the early numeracy scores. This raises the question, 'Why did mother's education not influence the early literacy scores too?'

The data below suggest home experiences may be influential, but the parents' educational backgrounds in themselves may not.

Numeracy in the home

According to the data collected in the main caregiver interviews about 'What?' and 'How?' children engaged with reading, writing and number, both groups were very similar. However, more of the comparison children did numeracy-related activities – such as counting, singing counting songs, using numbers in cooking, and learning to tell the time – at home. The comparison children also did a larger number of extra things with numbers (six categories, whereas the schema children did four).

Parents of comparison children reported the following activities: games/puzzles, using phone numbers, adding and subtracting, answering questions involving numbers, handling money and recognizing number symbols. Schema children did the first three activities, plus understanding patterns. These data show that there were a greater number of number experiences in the home for comparison children. In the main Competent Children study, children who explored more diverse mathematical experiences did better also.

There are many similarities between the two groups of children in the set of data about reading in the home. However, a wider range of people read to schema children, and more of these children read signs and brand names and looked at stories.

Home experiences can have a positive influence on children's numeracy and literacy scores. Phillips *et al.* (2002) in New Zealand, and Siraj-Blatchford and Sylva in England, have found this too. Siraj-Blatchford and Sylva (2004: 726) explain that in one of their case studies, it was the parents demonstrating 'proactive behaviour towards their children's learning' and providing a 'potent home-based pedagogy' that was cognitively effective.

The measure used

Third, the research instrument focused on children being able to identify categories, and it covered quite complicated mathematical ideas. However, it did not tap children's schematic actions associated with, for example, circles and spatial order schemas. Thus, there could have been a mismatch with the research instrument.

Discussion ■

With this small sample, the explanations for the better scores for schema children can only be speculative. In addition, the patterns in the findings could be regarded as surprising given the imperfect understanding of schema theory by most of those involved and the many constraints on the teachers putting the theory into practice.

Constructivist learning theory and research (for example DeVries and Kohlberg 1987; Worthington and Carruthers 2003; Nuthall 2007) suggest that there are a number of conditions and pedagogical approaches that improve young children's learning. They can be summarized as: Context, Content, Coordination with Parents, and Co-construction, and the cognitive processes of Recognition, Recall and Coordination. (With some linguistic playfulness – but with an underlying seriousness – it is possible to start each with a **'C'**).

Teachers need to:

• provide a child-centred *Context* with a relaxed classroom culture and flexible time use so children can self-select experiences and

experiment with things in their own ways to construct their own learning. In addition, the visual arts offer more opportunities for repeating experiences but with different media;
* have a good grasp of the *Content* of schemas as well as the concepts that are formed by children as a result of their explorations of clusters of schemas (see also Bransford *et al.* 2000; Johnston 2005);
* *Coordinate* with parents to discuss the threads in children's thinking and learning, and plan ways that children with a shared interest in a schema could coordinate their play (see also Whalley 2000; Meade 2007);
* *Co-construct* ideas and extend children's thinking through interactions where adults are also involved with learning associated with the child's interest (see also Meade 2007).

There is plenty of research to confirm that better staff–child interaction ratings in schema centres make a difference for children. These interactions are important for:

* the nourishment of *re-Cognition*; for example, by reflecting back in words to children what they are doing and may be thinking;
* assisting children to *re-Call* prior experiences that relate to their current thinking, pointing out cumulative threads of actions and thinking, and thereby helping them to consciously consolidate a cognitive structure;
* helping children to *Coordinate* different ideas to develop concepts.

Re-cognition, recall and coordination are thought processes that could be – and were – supported by pedagogical processes in the schema centres.

All these elements are important to support cognitively competent children to extend their thinking further and deeper. The presence of some of these elements was sufficient to produce enhanced scores on a range of competencies at the time the children began school. By age 8, the schema children had not maintained their comparative advantage – the intervention was not intense or long enough.

The teaching processes

Context

The centres' philosophy statements and other qualitative data indicated that all four centres – schema and comparison – operated child-centred curricula where children were able to pursue their interests.

The opportunities for children to explore the schemas that fascinated them were numerous and varied, although excursions, which can provide extension studies of existing schemas or trigger an interest in new schemas, were infrequent in the New Zealand centres.

The children could consume a rich 'diet' of experiences from the materials and experiences provided within the centres, including plenty of open-ended resources like sand. A variety of visual arts materials and blocks was also commonplace. These resources not only afford a rich diet, but challenge – children can move onto multiple pathways for representing their ideas in the abstract or for creating new ideas. Worthington (1996, cited in Worthington and Carruthers 2003: 41) found that records of play with these types of resources had the highest percentages of 'cognitively challenging' minutes.

Content

Content involves two aspects: curriculum content and teachers' content knowledge. It was the curriculum content that received most attention from the teachers. Imaginative enhancements and additions were made to equipment and materials. Teachers' content knowledge is also important (Farquhar 2003; Johnston 2005).

Data were not collected on the adults' knowledge of the content of children's thinking. In retrospect, it would have been valuable to have recorded more details about how teachers talked knowledgeably about content, especially when children were thinking about schemas. If the children pursue their thinking about schemas through to the level of scientific concepts – such as the concepts of lever and piston action or of trees branching (all of which can be developed by exploring 'connecting' schema) – then the adults themselves need to have an understanding of those concepts or, at least, be prepared to learn more about them alongside the children.

Coordination with parents

Parents were informed about schemas from the beginning of the project, and could relate to the threads in their children's thinking. In both schema centres, the staff were sharing knowledge about the children's schemas with parents intermittently, mostly when children were delivered to or picked up from the centres or parents read wall charts about children's schemas or in the portfolios the children brought home. Parents also sometimes told staff about schemas they noticed, especially at the workshops. This was low in intensity compared with the Wilton Playcentre.

Co-construction

Adults have a role to play in enriching and extending children's thinking by adding relevant resources and by extending the child's thinking through conversations about their experiences. Adding materials are easily within the adults' reach; for example, for children with a spiral scheme of action, adding dye to water and stirring, cooking pinwheel scones, playing outdoor games involving winding and unwinding actions, and making spiral wind-socks. But are these additions sufficient to embed concepts? Few involved co-construction in more complex learning that came near to the co-construction observed at the Wilton Playcentre.

Adult–child interactions and their effect on cognitive development

Re-cognition

Earlier in this report, there is reference to young children 'coming to know'. Elsewhere, Meade (1994) has called these re-cognition processes 'each time a child perceives a schema a little differently, she is re-cogniting'. The qualitative and the time-interval data indicate that the teachers made numerous adjustments to materials so that the schema children were afforded new opportunities to explore their schemas.

A more structured curriculum approach than that observed in any of the four centres may have limited the opportunities for children to rework their understanding; that is, limited their opportunities for re-cognition.

Adults in schema centres spent more time in conversation with the children than adults in the comparison centres. However, teachers' use of language to enhance re-cognition was minimal: in the qualitative data, there were few reports of adults talking about what the children were *thinking about* (*the form of their thoughts* as opposed to the *subject* of their art and constructions). When they did, they gave children words; for example, 'grid' to go with their explorations, they affirmed habits of mind such as curiosity, they assisted children's long-term memory development (Nuthall 2007), and helped children create explicit memories drawn from their implicit memories. Social mediation is important. Unfortunately, all too often the language interactions recorded in the Competent Children sub-study were superficial, such as 'Tidy up.'

Recall

The High/Scope curriculum (Schweinhart and Weikart 1986) is based on a constructivist approach. All four centres in this study had many High/Scope features, but not the particular cognitive process built into its daily programme: recall. Children in High/Scope settings are expected to start each day with a plan for a special activity, and at the end of the session groups of children sit with an adult and recall how their special activity progressed. ('No progress' is an acceptable answer.) The Competent Children action research data contain few examples of the teachers deliberately asking children to recall either content or schemas. There has been a marked increase in conversations that recall prior learning in New Zealand early childhood services since then, through their documentation in children's Learning Stories (Carr 2001).

Coordination

Assimilation and coordinating thinking processes help children to shape concepts in their minds. These processes, and thought structures, are necessary for more advanced abstract thinking. For example, as children are exploring the 'containing' schema, their understanding of 'capacity', 'volume', 'space', 'inside' and 'inclusion' can connect in their heads. The study revealed the very worrying fact that the teachers did not appear to be assisting children work at this more complex level. No more than five examples of teachers and children talking >thinking >talking were recorded. It can only be supposed that parents did talk in the abstract with their children.

Why did the schema children perform better?

The schema children's better performance is likely to be the consequence of centre curriculum changes, particularly changes embracing context and re-cognition.

Child-centred programmes with ready access to materials are important, because they allow children to construct a lot of knowledge about schemas for themselves – and they did. For example, the teachers did little to alter the regular curriculum for Stephanie and Susan, yet they found many ways to discover more about 'containing'.

However, as the context in the schema centres was little different from that in the comparison centres, differences in schema-centre results are probably not related to the child-centred approach. Nonetheless, a relaxed context was important tor all children to develop an understanding of schemas. The materials enrichment in the schema centres appeared to be a significant factor, especially since the additional materials were carefully chosen to fit the children's schema fascinations.

The second success factor was probably to do with the changes to adult–child interactions in the schema centres, where the teachers were targeting individual children for special observations and curriculum innovation. The nine children were more prominent in the teachers' consciousness during the six months the researchers and staff were studying their schema development.

In addition, the teachers' efforts to coordinate with parents, and the likelihood of the parents providing recall, re-cognition and coordination-of-thoughts experiences relating to schemas probably contributed to the differences too. A common theme in outcomes studies is that where parents have been involved in their children's early childhood education the children benefit more. The nature of the parent–child relationship changes when parents understand more about how young children learn (Whalley 2000; Mitchell *et al.* 2004). For example, Sam's parents changing their perspective about his tying chairs together (see Chapter 3) involved a switch from seeing this behaviour as naughty to seeing it as Sam learning about 'connection' and the physics of tension, among other things.

The role of parallel play in cognitive development

The greater proportion of time spent by the schema children in parallel play raises interesting questions about its role in cognitive development. Parallel play affords opportunities to observe other children's actions that are useful for developing one's own understanding of schemas, and of people, places and things more generally.

The Wilton Playcentre schema study

The Wilton Playcentre project was markedly different from the Competent Children sub-study. Two research associates joined the practitioner-researchers for the purpose of finding out more about schema learning in a setting where use of schema theory was well integrated into everyday practice. Not many early education services in New Zealand use schema learning theory, which is one of the reasons why the Wilton Playcentre was chosen for the centre of innovation programme. One of the aims of its research was to investigate

Photo 4.1 Learning from peers through parallel play.

what ways understanding of schema [theory] enable parent educators to support, extend and enrich children's learning at home and in the Wilton Playcentre.

The fact that the parent educators in the Wilton Playcentre are the children's parents provided a unique opportunity to study children's schemes of action and schemas in their most important micro-worlds. As most children start attending from infancy (with their parents) and continue through to school age, there was a further opportunity to study children's schemas across time and in mixed aged groups (infants to rising 5-year-olds).

The Wilton Playcentre schema study did not assess outcomes for children using quantitative research measures. There was no possibility of comparing these children with another group of children, as the Wilton Playcentre was treating itself as a case study. Its focus was on describing children's schemes of action and schemas, and on adults' pedagogical processes at home and in a licensed early education setting in relation to these schemas. Some qualitative data were gathered on the effects of these schema-informed teaching processes.

Playcentres could be described as part of the progressive education movement. They draw on ideas from Piaget, Vygotsky, Dewey and a New Zealand philosopher, Gwen Somerset, who all said that education should be child-centred, active and interactive, and involve family and community. Children's interests form the basis of curriculum emphases in Playcentres. It was an easy step for the Wilton Playcentre parent educators to make use of schema theory as one way of working with children's interests during the early education sessions. It was another easy step for schema theory to be taken home, as home was often where children's schemes of action are very apparent.

Playcentres run as parent cooperatives. Everyday functions are carried out by the children's parents, including the educator role. The Playcentre infrastructure provides a solid base of support, which includes systems and structures, policies, position descriptions, resources like libraries, and a within-centre education programme for adults. The Wellington Playcentre Association (regional governors), provide policies, training and professional development, equipment depots, and support personnel.

Framing conditions to support learning

As part of their research as a centre of innovation, the Wilton parent educators were asked what conditions in the Playcentre encouraged children to talk and think about their experiences. They could respond by talking about learning in general, not just schema learning. Parents named the good adult to child ratios, and then described how they took advantage of the ratios: listening to what children are saying and responding to them, documentation on and discussion about story boards (a page on the board about each child's current interests), using digital photos as discussion prompts, and supporting children to express how they feel. They also talked about arranging equipment and materials to fit the interests of different children. They discussed barriers and enablers at end-of-session evaluation meetings so that they could address any barriers and build on good features. After seeing the preliminary rating scale results in the centre of innovation action research, parent educators increased the frequency of open-ended questions.

Exploration of materials

Parent educators consciously set conditions that would extend and enrich schema learning. Their reports suggest that plans were formalized when 'certain children had an interest in common. Quite often the team uses interest in schemas for group planning, e.g., potions for lots of transformers' (Mitchell *et al.* 2004: 32). Core processes were knowing about children's schema learning and development, and knowing how to act on that theoretical knowledge.

Let us provide an illustration. A fascination with 'enveloping' schemes of action had been noticed by the mothers of Josie and of Nicholas, both in the Wilton Playcentre and at home. The excerpts in the text box from the journal kept by Josie's mother, Nikolien, demonstrated an understanding of her daughter's dominant schemas. They also showed her close understanding of Nicholas, who is not her own child. She was aware that both children were coordinating two schemas; namely, enveloping and transforming.

One day, the parent educator team at the Wilton Playcentre planned wrapping presents as an activity because these two children were constantly involved in this scheme of action. The adults put out objects to be wrapped and a variety of wrapping paper as well as scissors and sticky tape. Another day, they supplied strips of newspaper – enough for a child to hide underneath and jump up, or to hide another child. Nikolien's journal describes some additional ways the team provided fresh opportunities for children to repeat patterns of actions. The team provided continuity of experiences that would enrich the children's understanding of 'enveloping' and associated mathematics concepts across days or weeks, *and* they attended to young children's thirst for novelty in how they can experience 'enveloping'.

Nikolien's research journal

Josie and Nicholas do lots of 'enveloping'. They like to wear the dragon hoods and cloaks. Josie also likes to wrap her dolls in blankets, cover her tummy with flannels in the bath, stuff things into bags and carry them about, and she adores the barrel swing too. Nicholas also loves things like covering his hands and toys in messy gloop. Nicholas makes huts at home with cushions.

Both Nicholas and Josie have a strong interest in 'transforming', and like lots of mixing, messy play and baking. Because there are a group of children with these interests, our team tries to include something for them every week – either an enveloping thing like wrapping, tents, mosquito nets hanging, huts, big boxes; or something like gloop, finger paint or potions. Both Nicholas and Josie like to have their face painted, which explores both 'enveloping' and 'transforming' schemas. Yesterday, they both wanted to be dragons. Josie often chooses to be a tiger.

Nicholas was talking to me yesterday about how he paints his Mummy face, and that I don't have my face painted!

(Mitchell *et al.* 2004: 33)

Melissa, Nicholas's mother, supported his interest in 'enveloping' at home by helping to build a lot of huts with cushions, or forts with the table and chairs and a blanket – thereby extending his thinking into mathematical concepts related to size and capacity. Here we have examples of his parents behaving like those in the Competent Children sub-study that had good results. Nicholas's parents were providing a wide range of mathematics experiences, although we do not know if they were using mathematical language at the same time.

Social mediation

Nicholas and Josie had many adults attuned to the threads of ideas that interested them, in particular their parents and the team of educators at the Wilton Playcentre. The adults knew what schemas these two children liked to explore in their respective homes, as well as at Playcentre. They were aware that the adults knew about their ideas – the final sentence in the journal entry demonstrates Nicholas's confidence that Nikolien would understand his thinking. He chats to her about mothers and face paint, expecting her to follow his thinking. And she does follow the link, otherwise she would not have noted it in her research notebook.

Coordination of schemas

Worthington and Carruthers (2003) use the metaphor of schemas as thought 'footstools' for more complicated mathematical ideas.

Very early schemas can combine together, for example:

- horizontal *schema – carefully lining objects up horizontally*
- connecting *schema – lining objects up, one touching the other*
- number *schema – putting numbers to objects but not necessarily in the standard way. Children use numbers in everyday talk.*

Eventually all these schemas can work together to produce counting.

(Worthington and Carruthers 2003: 37)

We have little early education research on the topic, but linguists like Jean Mandler talk about language schemas in young children. These schemas coordinate so children can use more complicated language. The author of *Videatives Views* (2007) shares his or her observations of toddlers' fascination with language sound patterns: 'words' working together to produce 'sentences':

Before children begin to pronounce words they begin to 'pronounce' word-like sounds. If you listen for a while you will realise that these sounds are strung together into a small number of sentence-like patterns used repeatedly. And if you watch ... children orient to each other as they make these sounds.

Coordination between settings

The research at the Wilton Playcentre provides unique insights into coordinated schema learning at home and in an early childhood education setting. The Wilton Playcentre final research report notes that once the parent educators became familiar with schema theory and writing narrative assessments, they were able to make learning progressions more visible (van Wijk *et al.* 2006: 46).

The following section uses two examples of continuity and progressions of schemes of action between home and the Playcentre presented in the Wilton report. The excerpts are from case studies researched by two parents: Rosa written by her mother Rebecca (in van Wijk *et al.* 2006: 46–51), and Keir by his mother Sarah (in van Wijk *et al.* 2006: 61–5).

Rosa was almost 2 years of age when her case study was written. She had been at the Wilton Playcentre since 2 months of age, initially because of her older sister.

It is her second home and she treats it as such. . . . She exhibits a number of schema interests but her most dominant is a trajectory one, particularly its vertical aspects.

From an early age she has enjoyed watching things that move. We first observed her excitement when she was watching balls and anything that moved. (Rebecca, Rosa's mother)

Rebecca's narrative 'shows Rosa's progression from keen climber, to able climber and on to use "complex functional dependence" ideas to achieve an otherwise unattainable goal.'

The accounts from home include Rosa insisting on walking up and down their 114 steps independently.

If I let her, she'd jump each one, but we've managed to reach compromise and she jumps at the bottom of each flight of steps – there are 10 flights.

In this, Rosa would be absorbing patterns when descending the flights of steps, and ideas about downward movement and speed (stepping versus jumping).

Rebecca also included a story about Rosa stepping from the back of the sofa at home onto the 'roof of a hut' made of sheeting draped over a couch and chair.

> She suddenly climbed onto the sheet. It began to slip under her weight but she continued to transfer her weight until the sheet was under too much stress. . . . By doing this, she experienced that fabric can give way under stress and something about how gravity works. She was pleased with resulting drop and happy rather than upset when she landed – her sister was less than pleased.

The able-climber anecdote captured Rosa climbing on the climbing frame at the Wilton Playcentre several times. Rosa wanted to practise climbing up, over and down, sometimes backwards, thus coordinating 'vertical dynamic' and 'spatial order' schemas.

The event that stretched Rebecca's thinking as well as Rosa's was when Rosa decided to continue viewing photos on the family laptop when it was put on the dresser to recharge.

> To get there, she had to pull out the CD drawer from the left side where the handle is and then go around the open drawer to the chair. She would have climbed on the chair and then onto the open drawer. At that point she could reach the computer that she opened by pushing the button to release the lid to resume where we'd left off. . . . To do this Rosa must have been able to put her knowledge of a number of things together.

This is an example of 'functional dependency' understanding and abstract planning.

Keir was aged 3 years 3 months when his mother, Sarah, wrote his case study. He had attended the Wilton Playcentre since his third birthday, having been at another playcentre from 3 weeks of age.

> Keir often seemed to use several interconnected schema interests to investigate a particular 'thread of thinking'. Four currently dominate: horizontal and vertical trajectory, enclosing/enveloping, sorting and ordering spatial patterns, and connecting.

By this age, Keir was 'showing signs of refinement and increasing complexity.' He was 'fascinated by things that have impressive independent propulsion; for example, fish, birds, kites, helicopters, trains and volcanoes.'

For at least eight months, Keir was very interested in volcanoes. They fed his various schema interests. Sarah summarized his progression in thinking.

Photo 4.2 Volcanoes in the sandpit.

From motor action:

- running and biking at top speed;
- being flown through the air by Dad;
- flinging himself off the couch;
- running through the rain;
- experimenting with the movement of objects.

To symbolic representation:

- drawings (e.g., of waterfalls, slides and volcanoes erupting and models of volcanoes in the sandpit, hydrophobic sand and sawdust)

To abstract thinking:

- fantasy play involving erupting volcanoes;
- retelling facts from books read to him;
- understanding the difference between magma and lava.

Discussion

Without the understanding of schemas and noting schemes of action in the home, Rosa's climbing frame incident at the Wilton Playcentre would have been of little interest. When the schemes of action to do with the dynamic vertical schema at home and the Playcentre were coordinated, it became very apparent that Rosa was exploring ideas concerned with height (see also Nutbrown 2006: 60–2). Noting this, her interest in Joe and Simon at the Playcentre, who were nearly 5 years old, became meaningful. 'She was captivated by their amazing block structures . . . Knowing children's schema fascinations can help adults bring children with similar schema interests together.' (Rosa's mother)

Keir was fascinated by dynamic vertical too, but coordinating his schemas showed that he was exploring ideas to do with force and movement. He was also interested in the causes of changes in the properties of materials.

His mother, Sarah, noted the value of observing at home and other settings to identify children's coordinated actions, and of adults input into children's interests:

> These observations highlight connectivity and continuity between Keir's home and crèche, and home and playcentre. They also showed how adult extensions of Keir's interest in volcanoes served to fuel his interest and increase . . . his working theories on volcanoes.

SCHEMA INTERESTS AND EARLY LITERACY AT THE WILTON PLAYCENTRE

Six case studies of children at the Wilton Playcentre are presented to illustrate how schema fascinations link with and support early reading and writing literacy. The role children take in shaping the curriculum and the importance of adult–child interactions in enriching literacy at Playcentre and at home are described.

The context for the start of the case study data-gathering in 2004 was a 'make-over' of the Wilton Playcentre environment. Earlier data from an action research cycle in 2003 showed the environment rated only average on a 'print rich' scale. The parent educators took action – changing the environment and their pedagogy. They created an area devoted to writing with easier access to writing tools and materials; and also provided these and books in many areas of play, and a magnetic board for stories and children's names. They improved the displays of children's art and added text. Photos of children playing were accompanied by descriptions in the Māori language. Examples of children's mark-making were recorded and later analysed for links to their schema interests. Pedagogically, parents integrated literacy and numeracy meaningfully into the children's lives.

The changes 'sparked a spiral of enthusiasm with adults adding complexity and challenge to play, and children having the opportunity to further explore their interests and schemas in relation to literacy experiences' (Bulman *et al.* 2005: 12).

Early literacy

Early or emergent literacy includes such varied components as children's development of language, understanding the conventions of print; acquiring knowledge of letters which relates directly to [children's] later ability to decode words. A basic aspect of this skill is the awareness that letters have names and are associated with sounds.

(Landry and Smith 2006: 135)

Emergent literacy has several faces as seen in children's communication through their representations such as mark-making, early writing, pretend reading, telling stories, singing songs and fantasy play. Bruce (2005: 115) adds sign language, mathematical symbols, and musical and dance notation as further examples of different kinds of symbolic representation.

Brought together, print saturated environments rich in opportunities for the actions listed above, and complementary adult interactive strategies, will support literacy development at home and at the Wilton Playcentre. A print-rich environment is a factor found to have a sustained impact on child outcomes in the Competent Children longitudinal research project (Wylie 1996, 1999, 2004).

A word about mark-making

Whitehead (2001: 52) maintains that young children's first investigations of print and first attempts to use written symbols are the earliest stages of literacy and they do not involve real reading and real writing. She says that mark-making involves both creativity and communication and, to some degree, permanence: all components of literacy. Worthington and Carruthers (2003), in their book about mathematics, use the concept of children having 'a hundred languages' that they can choose from to express their own meaning. Mark-making is one of these languages. They found that through using mathematical symbols children furthered their mathematical learning:

The content the children explore through their early marks and the meaning they make are of the utmost importance. At the same time the function and form of children's early mark-making can be seen to develop in tandem with the content, if their schema interests are viewed as relating to their early writing.

(Worthington and Carruthers 2003: 56)

Children's early mark-making will not look like conventional writing and is often seen by adults as random scribbling of little consequence.

They may combine their letters, numerals and drawings, seeing no need to separate them but knowing that they are all symbols for communication. These marks need to be appreciated as 'intentional efforts by children to create and share meaning' (Worthington and Carruthers 2003: 55). Children use a variety of non-conventional marks in different ways to communicate in emergent writing, 'Children start with a scribble or a bit more and tell you about what was written' (Worthington and Carruthers 2003: 64). Through their acquaintance with a diversity of print and initial writing, they are learning an immense amount about reading.

Children make their own important discoveries that marks represent and convey meaning. In her novel *Rosetta*, Barbara Ewing (2005) writes beautifully of mark-making and the difference between child meaning and adult meaning in relation to symbols.

Rose is a child who loved her father reading to her the fairy-tale of Princess Rosetta who married the King of the Peacocks:

> She believed she was named after this princess. 'It's me! It's me!' she would cry. One day her mother took her up to the light airy drawing room and there: Rose held her first quill and with her mother guiding her hand she made the particular special marks that showed the letter R.
>
> 'We are drawing in the drawing room,' said Rose in delight.
>
> 'No, this is not drawing', said her mother, smiling, 'I am teaching you to write. This is writing, making words.'
>
> 'Writing, making words,' said Rose in awe.
>
> Soon the next day could not come quickly enough . . . Very soon Rose had the idea of making her own marks, not the R and the O and the S and the E that her mother formed.
>
> 'Why cannot I write like this, Mama?' she would ask, drawing a small rose. Her mother looked puzzled. 'It is me! Rose!'
>
> 'But this is not writing. It does not say anything,' her mother protested, laughing, 'though it is indeed very lovely.'
>
> 'It does say something,' insisted Rose. 'The star says "my mama" to me. Because you are beautiful, like a star. It is my writing. I am writing my way.'
>
> (Ewing 2005: 7)

The Wilton Playcentre case studies ◼

The children and their mothers are:

- Matthew (born 6/1/03), and Michelle;

- Isabelle (born 25/ 8/02), and Mary;
- Keir (born 26/2/02), and Sarah;
- Nyah (born 14/10/00), and Martha;
- Joe (born 25/9/00), and Lily;
- Kaitlyn (born 22/9/00), and Helen.

All six have siblings and two parents living at home. Three of the children – Matthew, Isabelle and Keir – have been written about in the report, *Transforming Learning at Wilton Playcentre* (van Wijk *et al.* 2006). Those case studies had a slightly different focus from these present ones because they were for a wider action research cycle focused on adults' open-ended questions and sustained conversations, as well as the emergent literacy of *all* the children. The case studies in this chapter consider the literacy development of the above three children in greater depth. In 2007, Pam Cubey interviewed their mothers again. She also examined the children's fuller portfolios to extend our understanding of schemas and literacy learning, and garnered further material from an unpublished report written by Wilson and Bulman in 2005. Her methods for the other three case studies – Kaitlyn, Nyah and Joe – were the same.

Our analysis of data showed that the six children generally first showed an interest in reading and/or writing selected letters and numbers that were connected to their schema interests. Those children who had strong 'circular' schema interests first took an interest in symbols such as 'a', 'o', '3' and '8'. Those drawn to 'M', 'W', 'T', 'L', '4' and '7' were fascinated by 'lines' and 'trajectories'. It has to be acknowledged, however, that letters and numbers in their name and age were often first in popularity.

These findings are from a small number of children, and are worthy of follow-up research.

> Our own names are full of meaning for us – they reflect our self esteem and sense of place in the world. Personal names are the first sets of known sounds and symbol combinations with which children feel totally confident. This gives them some very powerful insights into the nature of the written language system.
>
> (Whitehead 2001: 58)

We also found a different sort of literacy-related thread in their thinking – their realization that marks can 'stand for' something else. The children were 'coming to know' and understand the concept of *representation* (see also Bowman *et al.* 2000; Roskos, with Hanbali, *c.* 2002).

Three 'trajectory' boys ■

Matthew

Matthew has attended the Wilton Playcentre from birth. From an early age, his dominant schema interests have been 'rotation', 'circularity' and 'dynamic trajectory'. 'Figurative straight lines' and 'dynamic line' schemas were evident later.

As a toddler:

> He made sustained attempts to produce a circular scribble, employing strategies such as using paint pot lids for a circular shape, getting other people . . . to draw circles for him, and lots of practice before he produced continuous circular scribbles, describing them as 'circles' and 'spirals'. (*Michelle*)
>
> (Wilson *et al.* 2005: 23)

At age 1 year 11 months his drawings had representational ideas, he enjoyed 'writing' his name on his artwork and joining in when his mother was writing. Matthew (2 years 2 months) made his own book, sticking in photos of himself on a trip to the worm bin. He told an educator to write, 'Here is the worm bin' for each photo, adding his marks alongside.

Photo 5.1 Matthew in the middle of a strong throw.

Michelle said that he noted the differences between 3s, 8s and 5s, and circular letters and shapes, yet took longer to learn the straight line letters like 'M' for Matthew. He was interested in straight line letters by 2 years 7 months.

Charles, his father, wrote of walking home together:

> We walk home, stopping at all the letter boxes. Matthew points out '3' and '9' and asks me the other numbers, recognizing '5' as '2'. Then he notices a car number plate, very excited to see an 'M' – 'M' for 'Mattie.' 'M' for 'me.'
>
> I say 'M' is for Michelle and Mummy too. 'That's *my* "M" says Matthew. He asks me the other letters and numbers too. The next car has a "W" which he points out as an "M". I say it is an upside down "M", a "W". He is interested in an "F". I say "F" for fish, going back to a favourite alphabet puzzle. He is very excited to see another upside down "M" further on, an "F" for fish and an "O" like a circle'. Here his rotation and straight line trajectory interests are coming together.
>
> When spotting car number plates he became interested in the symmetry of 'M' and 'W', bending down to look up and see them reversed to 'W' and 'M'. He enjoyed the fact that the 'M' and 'W' in his name could be turned (rotated) to make the other letter. (*Charles*)

His parents were alert to signs of emerging mathematics knowledge. For example, Matthew at 2 years 5 months was helping Charles unload the dishwasher:

> He picked up a red container and asked where it went. I said, 'In the red box where the other plastic containers are.' Matthew disagreed and put it by a similar red container on the table and did the same with a third red container. Meanwhile, I'd been stacking plates. When I put a bowl on top of the plates Matthew objects and moves it to a new pile, then collects other bowls and adds them, with a continuous running commentary about making a pile of bowls ('vertical trajectory'). Then put the cutlery, knives, forks, spoons, teaspoons, in order: 'That goes there, that goes there, that goes there.' (*Charles*)

He showed a clear understanding of classification: sorting, ordering and matching things, important for reading. At the age of 4 he could form the alphabet and his name in New Zealand Sign Language (trajectory movement, and understanding *representation*). By 4 years 2 months he wrote his name, using 'T T M W', finding it easier to write 'WET' rather than 'DRY' on a sign he had made; favouring straight 'trajectory' lines over his earlier concentration on 'circular' marks.

Photo 5.2 Matthew painting his flag for his pirate pretend play.

He loved telling and acting out his imaginary tales about going to the moon or to Canada to see polar bears, using 'dynamic trajectory' words. He enjoyed rhymes, songs and stories – especially humorous ones, which he enjoyed retelling to his family at home. These are all important aspects of emergent literacy.

During his early Playcentre years, he was involved in energetic action, using symbolic representation, exploring functional dependency and recounting stories without physical prompts (abstract thought). By 4 years Michelle said he had a practical approach to literacy, asking about words and writing. He wrote if it served a purpose, but was not interested in writing for its own sake. He began school early in 2008.

Keir

Keir started attending a different Playcentre when 3 weeks old. He moved to the Wilton Playcentre at age 3 years; and attended a crèche three days a week. His schema interests included 'enclosing', 'connecting', 'rotation', 'transformation' and a strong interest in 'dynamic vertical trajectory'. (We described Keir's interest in volcanoes in Chapter 4.)

At 3 years 2 months, records showed Keir was particularly interested in 'rotation', 'enclosure' and 'trajectories'; he could recognize his name and wrote it for the first time on a card for his grandfather. About that time he sang the alphabet song right through non-stop.

> Keir did a production line of 14 drawings – commencing with Humpty Dumpty: a circle for face, eye, eye, mouth, belly button, hair, leg, leg, using 'rotational' marks for all the features: the first time for a really representational drawing of a person. He drew seven similar drawings. Twice he 'enclosed' Humpty in another circle. Then he suddenly became very energetic doing vigorous 'rotational trajectory' scribbles, while chanting. As his energy dropped, he changed to a lower, more controlled style and back to 'circular, rotational' drawings, making sure the circles met up exactly. (*Sarah*)

Whitehead notes that 'children who appear to be scribbling wildly are often imitating the cursive writing they see adults doing' (2001: 57).

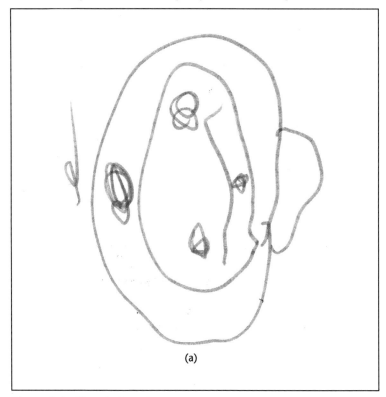

(a)

Figure 5.1a Humpty Dumpty.

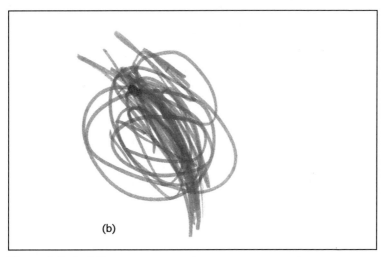

(b)

Figure 5.1b Scribbles.

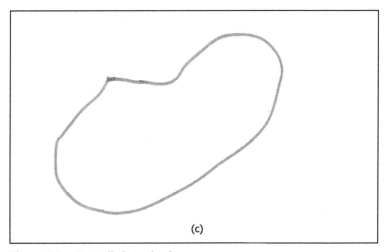

(c)

Figure 5.1c Controlled circular drawings.

A close relationship with Merryn (older sister) stimulated his interest in some schemas, as well as helping Keir develop his emergent literacy. They often used each other as resources, sharing ideas in co-constructing their play, and books they enjoy about living creatures.

Merryn shows Keir (3 years 4 months) how to do spirals. She carefully and very clearly describes to him what she is drawing.

Photo 5.3 Keir and Merryn reading.

'See now I've done it – you could do it too.' Keir draws some spirals and repeats the process to perfect his technique. He first draws very quickly, seeming to enjoy the flow, process and energy of the rotational movement, then quietly, slowly and carefully, draws three clear spirals and embellishes the drawing by incorporating an angler fish. He then acts as a resource for Merryn, who notices what he has drawn and decides to draw an angler fish too. (*Sarah*)

Merryn helped Keir grasp the first letter of a word schema. Keir aged 3 years 5 months and Merryn are in the car when Merryn thinks of words that begin with certain letters:

Merryn:	sw, sw, sw . . . swimming,
Merryn:	sw, sw, sw . . . sweetie. Then:
	Let's do M, no let's do W.
Keir:	w, w, w . . . water.
Merryn:	w, w, w . . . worm.
Keir:	w, w, w . . . watch. (Sarah)

Keir showed an increasing interest in the alphabet, sounds, writing and reading when Merryn brought her school work home.

Keir detected 'open continuous triangles' (a line schema) in relation to letter symbols at age 3 years 5 months when he wrote a Z, 'Hey, I can do a Z. I know I can do a Z with Lego.' He found a Lego manual and showed his mother a Z at the end of the alphabet page (finding his way through print). Three days later he made a 'Z' with magnetic rods; then he moved the rods to make a '5' (thereby demonstrating his recognition *and* production of numerals and letters). His favourite letters to draw were 'i' and 'j' ('dynamic straight lines'). By 4 years 6 months he wrote his name clearly with well-formed letters.

Keir's interest in 'straight and curved lines', 'enclosures', 'connecting' and 'space order' seen in his mark-making clustered together to enable him to write confidently. Sarah thought his schema explorations also gave him a sound base for solving mathematical problems. At the time of writing, he was well settled at school (age 5 years 8 months), and was an enthusiastic and competent reader and writer.

Joe

Joe attended the Wilton Playcentre from soon after birth and crèche from 1 year old. He explored many schema interests in a variety of ways. 'Vertical' and 'horizontal trajectories' were expressed through energetic motor actions and symbolically in concentrated block constructions. 'Trajectory', 'enclosing', 'enveloping', 'connecting' and 'rotation' clustered together in his beloved superhero play.

At age 3 years 9 months, Joe was at the magnetic board, matching letters and numbers by colour and shape. He was delighted when he found those that matched, and discussed the letters in his name and the beginning letters of names in his family. He became very excited to find '8' because his brother is 8.

Joe's fascination with the letters 'J', 'o', 'e', and numeral '8', have a direct relevance to him personally, and their curved component also indicated (or match) his fascination in 'circularity' and 'rotation'. A month later, Joe drew a number of circles: 'I need another piece of paper.' Then he drew many circles; then circles around the circles, followed by connected up and down strokes. 'This is how you make letters. I'm writing.' Here he makes the explicit connection between mark-making and representation (van Wijk *et al.* 2006: 30).

> In the past, Joe seldom used literacy materials at playcentre. When he was approaching four, we noticed him becoming very interested in the number of his age and in sounding out the letters of his name. I wrote his name and age on the computer and stuck it on his bed head as a surprise. He was very pleased to see it and showed each family member. (*Lily*)

Photo 5.4 Joe and Simon matching letters and numbers.

Joe showed an increased interest in numbers and letters around the time the literacy initiatives were introduced at the Wilton Playcentre:

> Joe is passionate about made up hero stories: he's had a Batman story almost every night for the past two years and often during the day he will ask for one. One day at playcentre he asked me to draw Batman for him. After some encouragement from me that he could do it, he drew an accurate representation: two eyes (circles), two verticals at the side of the head, two arms with claws, and two legs. When I asked if he wanted his name he firstly drew a back-to-front 'J,' which he then corrected, then an 'o' to the left of the 'J' and I wrote an 'e' also back-to-front in keeping with his idea. He realised the name was back-to-front ['spatial order'] and I helped him write it forwards. We took that drawing home and he showed me where to put it on his wall. (*Lily*)

This account illustrates the connection of Joe's innate forms of thought ('trajectory' schemas) and content (Joe's passion for superheroes and adventures) with feelings.

A series of photos around age 4 years 6 months showed Joe totally absorbed on his own, connecting different structures in the outdoor area with string, making a trail from one point to the next. Later in the

Figure 5.2 Joe's 'Incredible Hulk'.

session, the adult observer talked with him about these actions captured in photos.

Joe: I'm just tying up at playcentre. ('connecting')
Adult: Why is your trail so long?
Joe: I just like tying up. And then I cut it up. ('disconnecting')
There's no picture of my cutting up.

'Connecting' and 'disconnecting' are important schemas for learning to chunk strings of symbols into words.

Lily reported that now Joe is attending school, he likes mathematics and came to it more easily than to reading and writing. However, writing is his favourite thing when he has 'Something good to write about', for

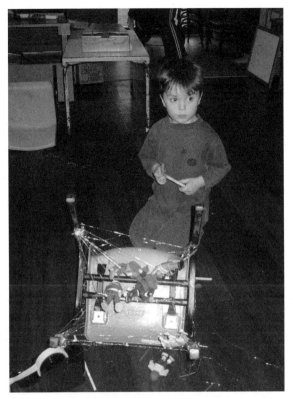

Photo 5.5 Joe connecting with string.

example Transformers (similar to his action heroes). Here he is like many boys, for example, Harry researched by Cath Arnold (2003).

The older Wilton Playcentre boys display exuberant, dynamic, 'vertical' and 'horizontal' schemas in their play, but also engaged in less vigorous precursors of literacy: being read to, telling their own stories, building with blocks and connecting things. Their mark-making involved action schemas – scribbling vigorously.

Barriball (1985) explains the value of outdoor play where children like Joe, Keir and Matthew can deeply explore, through movement, such mathematical ideas as boundaries, positions, viewpoints, routes, distances, size, shape and comparisons. She believes these are vital forerunners for a full understanding of most fields of mathematics. We found that schemas enriched by outdoor experiences to do with, say, position and direction, shape and comparison also helped to lay the foundations for writing and reading.

Three different girls

Isabelle

Isabelle began at the Wilton Playcentre when she was 15 months old. 'Rotation' was her first dominant schema fascination. It continued strongly, along with 'ordering', 'enclosing' and, later, 'layering'. Mary photographed Isabelle at the Wilton Playcentre at age 2 years 1 month using writing materials, easily accessed by a toddler because of the 'make-over' of the environment. She drew marks like letters and enclosed her work in another sheet of paper.

At 2 years 4 months Isabelle made orderly cuts along a piece of paper and lined up paper boxes. She made a little mark on each of five papers, took out five envelopes and placed one paper in each (1:1 correspondence). Two months later, Isabelle counted, '1, 2, 3, 4, 5' as she drew five circles in a line. At home at the blackboard, she said, 'I'll draw a big circle: I'm drawing a rainbow.' She was intent, focused and open-mouthed, wearing what came to be recognized as her 'schema face'.

'Rotation', 'rotation', 'rotation!' Isabelle is learning how her marks

Photo 5.6 Isabelle drawing big circles.

can represent something. She is also spotting things in her environment that appeal to her schema. As I write, she is rolling over the floor and singing the song 'There are ten in the bed and the little one said, roll over, roll over.' (*Mary*)

Isabelle at rising-3 years is not as attracted to the first letter of her name, as is common in many young children. 'A' is her most talked about and recognized letter; 'A' is for Aidan, her young brother.

Isabelle demonstrates some literacy awareness – in her left-to-right mark-making and her commentary as she paints, 'X Y Z'. She is very excited by [this] hand painting. With her marks she imitated formal writing when 3 years old, starting with small, fine, circular 'letters' and finishing with bold circular flourishes. (*Mary*)

A strong interest in books at this early age included many about vehicles with wheels – *Thomas the Tank Engine* interested her; also ballet stories with twirling dancers. A popular book was *Samuel Whiskers* or the *Roly Poly Pudding*. Sometimes she would talk about the 'roly poly pudding' as she wrapped herself in a rug and rolled on the floor.

By 3 years 8 months, Isabelle was increasingly interested in the magnetic board, forming letters and seeing her name. At 4 years 2 months she drew careful 'I's followed by deliberate letter-like marks. Her own 'I' is now important.

Notebooks fascinated her (and still do); she spent much time carefully filling each lined page with writing. The fine motor skills she had achieved are shown in the photo of her controlled and systematic mark-making (see Figure 5.3).

Isabelle at 4 years 4 months drew several detailed maps that she talked about. Mary thought they were a representation of their suburb. At the nearby bush reserve Isabelle took a map from the information centre and studied it as the family walked in the park.

About that time Isabelle went with Mary and her baby sister to a health centre where Orla was weighed and measured. Isabelle drew 'A measuring chart for how long Orla had grown.'

I find it interesting how the measuring lines on her chart are not linear like a ruler but circular! More 'core and radial' too, plus 'inside–outside' or 'enclosure' with squiggles on the inside of the chart. It shows too her distinction between drawing and writing. I think the letters at the bottom are random (despite the appearance of a word). At her request I read them out. I asked her what she had written. She said 'What you said.' I think she is interested that letters can mean something in terms of a certain sound. (*Mary*)

Four months later Isabelle made two books at the Wilton Playcentre:

'Going to the Zoo' and 'Moving House'. She told Mary about her pictures in the latter one, bringing together many familiar schemas:

> A lovely picnic place so they don't have to go out for picnics . . .
> Hanging up a lovely basket that they made together.
> A lovely little climbing frame that we could climb any day but on cold days we had to dress up really warm.
> A little path that went 'inside and outside'.
> Two bridges that went 'round and round' and 'under and under'.
> A nice long, long race track.
> A lovely nice warm cooking thing.
> A twirly-whirly bed. (*Mary*)

Isabelle's progress in literacy developed in tandem with her schema interests. 'Rotation', 'circular', 'ordering' and 'sequencing' schemas formed a cluster. At first, all explorations of her dominant schema fascination of 'rotation' were explored through her *motor actions*; for example, turning handles, making things spin, whirling in her 'circle dress', and re-enacting the 'roly poly pudding'. Her musical role plays included 'Ten in the bed'. Her *symbolic representations* reflected 'rotation', 'ordering' and 'sequencing' – she drew countless circles and arcs, imitating formal

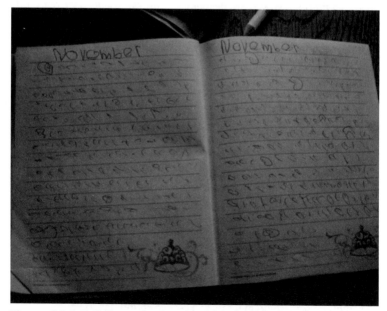

Figure 5.3 Isabelle's notebook with predominance of circular marks and layered paper on top.

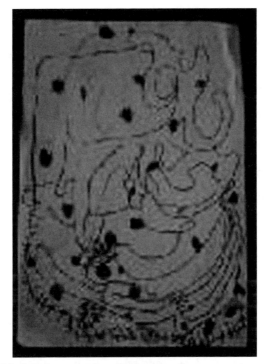

Figure 5.4 Isabelle's map of the neighbourhood.

writing, especially of letters and numbers with a round form. In her many notebooks she became a writer, almost as if she was doing shorthand, showing well-developed fine motor coordination as she made marks flow along the narrow lines.

By 4 years 11 months, Isabelle could think in the abstract to draw a map of a familiar place, compose stories and translate her marks to read her book to someone special, her mother. At the time of writing, Isabelle was in her first term at school, when her writing shows she cannot seem to resist making letters like 'V' curvaceous like a 'U'.

Nyah

Nyah began at the Wilton Playcentre when she was 1 year old, and from 2 years 5 months also went once a week to crèche.

Nyah at age 2 years 10 months painted a picture and said, pointing to her writing, 'Look, this is "N" and this is "A", and this is my name.' She continued to work hard at perfecting her name and said confidently, 'I can spell my name: N Y A H, you see.' As for all six case study children, her name was very important to her.

Nyah enjoyed activities involving 'layering', 'enclosing', 'enveloping', 'ordering', 'transforming' and 'vertical and horizontal trajectories'. However, most patterns did not occur obviously enough for any to be identified as dominant schemas. We did not want to name a schema simply for the sake of applying a label to her actions. Nyah was actively and deeply engaged in play and explored ideas in many ways.

When, one day, Anne Meade suggested that Nyah might be fascinated with 'spatial relationships' and 'spatial order', the scales fell from our eyes. Re-examining records of her learning revealed her intense love of swinging high where she could see over the fence, surveying the surroundings from a different perspective, and her discussions with other children about being in rockets, blasting off, going to the sun and how they would get there. She had been exploring ideas of place and 'space relationships' associated with travelling (where people are going on journeys by different means, how long it takes to reach the destinations and how far away these are).

> Arguably, she has lifted her thinking to a higher level, understanding maps in abstract thought, not as a piece of paper.
>
> (Wilson *et al.* 2005: 16)

Martha recalled that 'spatial relationship' discussions often occurred while on car journeys to visit friends and relatives. Perhaps this interest began with going and coming between the connecting points of home and the Wilton Playcentre; in other words, with the dynamic schema of going from point A to point B, and 'back and forth'.

Nyah (4 years 6 months) became deeply involved with her Playcentre friends drawing treasure maps and using them to plot hidden treasure and joining in the hunt to discover it. She was a central participant in this extended map play, introduced it at crèche and carried it over to home where she continued map drawing and doing treasure hunts with Martha. The family extended this interest in 'spatial relations' by visiting the library to borrow relevant books.

Nyah has family in the USA, India and different parts of New Zealand, and regularly corresponds with them. This interest in 'connecting' to people in different places was extended in letter-writing activities at the Wilton Playcentre. Several of the children enjoyed writing and posting letters to each other and the parents would then deliver them to their home letter boxes. As Nyah replied to a letter to her friend Elliot, in the USA, Martha's open-ended questions engaged her in thinking about and articulating her ideas on how the letters are transported from one letter box to the other.

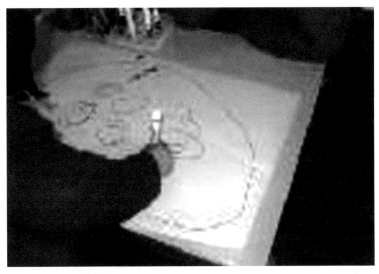

Photo 5.7 Nyah drawing a treasure map.

Photo 5.8 Nyah completes her letter to grandpa.

Children are learning much more about books and print because in all cases they are choosing the form of their books and print, and it becomes directly relevant to them.

(Wilson *et al.* 2005: 29)

Nyah gravitated to adults reading stories, 'reads' books with friends and took part in presentations of their pretend plays to an appreciative audience.

Before she started school, Nyah knew that thoughts and words can be represented in symbols and writing. Six months after starting school, Martha reported that Nyah was progressing very well with her reading and writing, and that sending letters to her grandparents in the USA and New Zealand had become a way of life. She was interested in the game of *Battleships*, which requires spatial visualization and in *Google Earth*. She is following her mother's interests – Martha studied geography at university and is the family map-reader and navigator.

Kaitlyn

Kaitlyn began at the Wilton Playcentre when she was 5 months old. Before she was 2 years old, Kaitlyn showed an interest in 'transporting', 'enclosing', 'rotation' and 'trajectory' schemas. By the age of 3 years 6 months her fascination with 'transformation' appeared, both of materials and herself. From this time on a dominant interest, evident in her roles in pretend play, was the rescuing theme, strongly supported by choosing stories that reflected that idea. Kaitlyn participated in the popular treasure hunt play, immersed as the treasure hunter and creating a story around her role.

Around the same time, one day Kaitlyn persisted in attaching a flat stick to a piece of paper. When asked if she wanted her name on it, she said, 'Yes, I'll draw my name . . . that's Kaitlyn. I love Mummy.' Kaitlyn understood that marks convey meaning (representation).

Kaitlyn, at age 3 years 10 months, was using strong strokes and dabs as she painted one day.

> I suggest she write about [her three paintings] so that other people can read about them. Kaitlyn is very enthusiastic and helps me with the letters. We sound them out: 'Some grass, a flower, a ring'. Kaitlyn is able to tell when letters are repeated in different words. I suggest we write her name and date – enthusiastic agreement – she tells me what letters come next. Here Kaitlyn continues to extend her recognition of the connections between oral and written language and between pictorial representations and written language. (*Mary*)

Helen introduced a pad and pencil into the game of shops that she and Kaitlyn were playing. Helen noted, 'I drew what I wanted to buy, the number and the word and Kaitlyn deciphered. Then she wanted to do the same herself.' On each of Helen's notes Kaitlyn drew her picture or wrote the item's name or wrote her own note with her number and letter for

Photo 5.9 Kaitlyn writes in the sand, 'No digging. Dead bird here.'

what she had drawn. Next they matched numerals to the shopping items. Helen noted, 'I was encouraging confidence and fun with literacy.'

As she grew older, rescuing and dramatic portrayal of known stories, and others invented by Kaitlyn and her friends, occurred daily at the Wilton Playcentre. At Kaitlyn's request, she and Helen dressed up as dragons.

> Kaitlyn said, 'I am called Spotty Dragon and you are called Drag Dragley'. They danced off to the sand-pit and built a dragon castle, using pipes as towers and Kaitlyn then made small castles to fit inside the tower. Kaitlyn said, 'Princess Fiona is inside the tower and needs to be rescued.' Rescue play ensued. (*Helen*)

Later, a Playcentre team member who had observed them initiated a story with dragons on the white board to connect the pretend play with some literacy actions.

> Kaitlyn and Jamie grew more and more excited as the story they helped to create unfolded. Towards the end of the story, Kaitlyn drew Princess Fiona on the board. 'I need to rescue Princess Fiona'; drew herself, and with a few magic words was transported inside the board.
>
> (Wilson *et al.* 2005: 14)

Photo 5.10 Kaitlyn and friends sharing story-telling.

Kaitlyn (4 years 11 months) initiated a favourite activity, a group story-telling, on her last day at the Playcentre before starting school. By then, she understood the concept of story formats. Kaitlyn, Emma, Nyah, Hazel and Keir sat in a cosy circle with Helen who suggested they all take turns in telling a story.

> Kaitlyn: 'I want to be the story teller.' She begins: 'It was a dog. The dog is going to chase the cat. So they went around all through the town to the dog centre and the man gave the dog a biscuit but the cat was really hungry'. With Helen's assistance Hazel continues the story. Kaitlyn isn't sure about the turn the story takes: 'But cats don't like bones!' With Helen's help she agrees it could be a small bone. As Nyah expands on the story, Kaitlyn waits. She is keen that everyone gets their turn, saying, 'Emma didn't tell.' when it looks like Emma may have missed out. Kaitlyn's turn: (we are now inside a castle): 'They see a big, big, big, big, big monster inside chasing mice and killing them'. Hazel expands on this. Kaitlyn, 'Now it's Keir's turn.' She yawns, she's tired but attentive. Emma leaves temporarily. Kaitlyn: 'Ooh, Emma's going away. Can I be the next person?' The story continues. (*Mary*)

Mary was feeding her baby nearby while observing and recording. Later, she reflected in writing on this episode:

Kaitlyn is very involved, despite appearing physically tired. She takes responsibility for ensuring that the rules of the game are followed and that everyone has their chance to participate. She grabs every opportunity to further her participation within the rules.

Mary detected schemas:

Perhaps Kaitlyn is 'transforming' her [schema] ideas into a story; e.g., 'transporting' and ['going through boundaries'] ideas. Helen ensures that less vocal children have a chance to contribute, facilitating the imagining, guiding participation, and confirming that the contributions are worthwhile.

Talking about the 'make-over' of the Wilton Playcentre environment, Helen said that Kaitlyn was absolutely ready to take full advantage of the new provisions of literacy tools in all areas of activity: the magnetic white board, clipboards, story-making, using pens, shopping, café servery, taking orders and counting out money, being a rescue fire-fighter and writing a fire report, making tickets for a bus ride, directing a drama, helping to make the post box and writing letters to her Playcentre friends. She became a confident emergent writer, keen to play at writing, and exploring and experimenting with different writing resources.

Now at school, Kaitlyn often has a splurge of reading many books at one sitting and reads in bed until 7.30 p.m. She has 14 chapter books that she enjoys rereading. She writes letters to her grandmother in England, impatient for a reply, and likes listening to her sister Emma's stories. Kaitlyn is still 'transforming' and rescuing, wanting things to be right for people.

Reflection on the role of the children in shaping the curriculum ∎

These six case study children were able to explore their schema interests, freely choosing what to play with, with whom and for how long. The dispositions of concentration, persistence, involvement, contribution and expressing ideas or feelings – important aims of *Te Whāriki, Early Childhood Curriculum* – were strong in all these children because of the pedagogical approach of the parent educators at the Wilton Playcentre. Their view of children as active and competent learners, and their interest in children's schemes of action, supported dispositional learning as well as learning relating to mathematics, science and literacy.

The children's passion for their dominant schemas helped to shape the content of the curriculum. Once the Wilton parent educators became competent at recognizing children's schemes of action, and the 'working theories' underlying them (*Te Whāriki*), they could draw on an additional mental framework (Hanna 2006) for developing the curriculum. They enriched the context and content of the curriculum, for example, with increased opportunities for mark-making experiences to assist children's '*re-cognition*', and helped children *coordinate* their mental processes in order to understand representation (see Chapter 4). They engaged in co-construction with individual children; for example, Mary learning with Isabelle about different ways to make marks to depict how baby Orla has grown. And they picked up on new enthusiasms of a group of children and organized extensions or projects around these interests over several sessions; for example, when maps came into the curriculum.

The Wilton Playcentre systems for communicating children's interests from one teaching team to the next – documentation on a whiteboard, in the session evaluation notes, on photo displays, and in individual learning stories – gave the following day's team indications of where they could build the curriculum around children's interests, and they provided fresh encounters relevant to children's schemas. Documentation was done on the day and there was an immediate pedagogical response at the next session. Parent educators reading the documentation from yesterday provided role models for the children, and triggered conversations among the team and with children that assisted their recall (memories) of prior experiences. These Playcentre systems channelled adults thinking about children's thinking. Data collection for the action research, focused on mark-making and sustained conversations, enhanced that thinking.

Although the examples linking schema interests to writing are only part of a bigger picture of their literacy learning at the Wilton Playcentre, data in these case studies show that actions triggered by the action research project resulted in more opportunities for children to explore and express themselves through their mark-making. Parents learned more about their own important role in the literacy processes, and became more confident and competent in supporting, extending and enriching their children's schema learning. Our follow-up study made emergent literacy even more visible.

A word about the toddlers

Many of the children had been at the Wilton Playcentre since infancy. As schema interests were detected when they were toddlers, it was often noticed that they enjoyed being near, watching and following older children who displayed similar schemas. Then they too would try their hand at doing figurative representations of their schemas, using pens and paint. They were attracted to the many opportunities for mark-making, which were freely available.

The parent educators became more alert to evidence of their toddlers' schema fascinations. Their philosophy of providing freedom of choice, space, time, accessible equipment and materials, and a relaxed attitude to 'messy' play assisted the schemas to cluster. Involvement in their children's early education ensured that extensions happened in play at home as well as at Playcentre.

Adult–child interactions enrich literacy in the centre and at home

Worthington and Carruthers (2003) believe that nurseries and schools cannot match the home as a learning environment, which provides a real and purposeful learning situation with an immense range of events that occur as a result of everyday living. The situations that children are exposed to are with people who know them, who share their background and common experiences.

The Wilton Playcentre parent educators, educating children in addition to their own, come to know many young children very well. The

Photo 5.11 Mixed age learning at the blackboard: Hazel, Kaitlyn and Nyah.

adults and children share more common experiences than occurs in settings with salaried teachers; for example, the children go to play at parent educators' homes. Playcentre children are very comfortable with a range of parents, and the Playcentre becomes like a second home – an extended family. The children wait at the end of sessions, and watch their parents talk together and write up session evaluations. In sum, the interactions and flow of information between the Playcentre and homes are numerous and diverse.

Nutbrown ([1994] 2006) observed that as children begin to pay attention to adults modelling the act of writing, they follow adult examples:

> They move their pen quickly across the page as they perhaps have seen their mother do when she writes a quick letter. They might produce a series of linear squiggles which represents the look of writing and, in the act, they get the *feel* of being a writer ... they assume the posture ... of a writer, write with intensity ... their faces show concentration and they 'write' with the certainty of focus and purpose.
>
> (Nutbrown 2006: 81)

Bruce confirmed the importance of children seeing adults 'writing for real' (2005: 147). Playcentre educators showed the children that adults like to write at the centre and at home; adults sometimes write carefully, and other times write rapidly. The Wilton Playcentre parents made mistakes at times as they wrote and the adults conveyed that that is alright. They also talked to children about their writing.

Athey ([1990] 2007) has said that without talking with children there is little information on whether children are investing their marks with meaning. An example from the Wilton Playcentre illustrates these points:

> After playing 'shop' with me in the Wendy House, Nyah (4 years 5 months) approached me with a piece of paper, saying 'I meant to give this to you in the shop'. (She gave customers pieces of paper, some with writing on). I asked her to read it to Isabelle. Nyah: 'I don't know what it says yet, but it says something.' Then, as if changing tack, 'It's a picture.' Together, with Isabelle looking on, we went through each symbol, identifying them as D, A, K, N, T, D and a square. I grabbed a piece of paper and scribbled notes for a possible Learning Story. Nyah asked: 'What are you writing?' I explained I was writing about our conversation so I could remember it for later. Isabelle (2.6) takes a piece of paper and the pencil I was using and writes her own

Photo 5.12 Mary and Isabelle writing at home.

version. Nyah clarifies: 'It's for Isabelle, it's not a story; it's a picture.' (*Mary, Isabelle's mother*)

Michelle (Matthew's mother), commented on Mary's observation:

> While Nyah learns more about writing she is also providing a model for Isabelle. Isabelle is learning some important things in this play from both Nyah and Mary. Nyah reinforces that papers have messages, when Mary and Nyah discuss the specific form of the letters Isabelle watches Mary form the letters and explain to Nyah that she is recording a conversation so that she can remember it later. She shows just how much knowledge she has picked up through methods like this by writing her own version, she uses the same style paper as Nyah and Mary's pencil, she shows clearly that writing goes in horizontal lines and that it is made up of individual symbols. It suggests that Isabelle has confidence in herself that her writing too is of value.

In the next example, the Wilton Playcentre accident record book served a dual purpose:

Bella has two prickles in her foot and insists Mum remove them but Mum's not here. Several different solutions are tried but to no avail. Bella is upset. Sue suggests we write about it in the 'concerns' book and tape the prickles in for our end of session evaluation so that something can be done about it. In combination with a biscuit Bella is happy for me to take out the prickles and keenly interested to see the writing in our concerns book with the prickles beside it. (*Michelle: recorder and prickle remover*)

Children learn a great deal about the importance of print, and literacy by watching adults who demonstrate they value these activities. Bella understood the power of print, and adults helped her through a time of being upset by drawing on that understanding and writing the event down.

Incidents such as the two described above were shared with the children's own parents, thus providing information that could be recalled later in the family. These home conversations about daily experiences, both past and present, are important. Reliving what occurred in centre sessions, making connections between the places, finding out the stories the children enjoy in each setting (which are often related to their schema interests) and retelling them together provide rich literacy experiences. Landry and Smith (2006) found that early literacy experiences at home are important predictors of later literacy skills.

Conclusion

Their children's schema learning fascinated the Wilton Playcentre parents. The parents of the six children we studied in depth had continued to reflect on their children's schema interests and to keep thoughtful records of their progress many months after the centre of innovation research was completed. These family records are treasured artefacts of both the children's and the parents' learning, a special family autobiography. The participation of the whole family in thinking about children's thinking and learning has been profoundly changed.

6

CHILDREN'S LEARNING AND PROFESSIONAL LEARNING

Chapter 6 discusses the biological and socio-cultural aspects of schema learning. A model indicating the relationship between schemas in the subconscious and conscious explicit and autobiographical narrative memories is developed. It demonstrates the importance of teacher mediation. The ways children learn best from the environment, from their peers and from adults are further examined. The book ends with a discussion on fostering progression in thought.

Reflective questions for readers to discuss with colleagues complete this chapter.

Schemas – the core of developing minds

Much has been written in the last decade about social learning and the cultural nature of human development. Most early childhood authors refer to biological aspects of learning in passing, acknowledging that 'nature and nurture dance together'; the discourse emphasizes socio-cultural learning. Yet, young children are fascinated by 'things' in the material world and want to learn more about them.

Gopnick *et al.* (1999: 83) state that young children 'are born knowing a great deal, they learn more, and we are designed to teach them' about things, as well as about people and language. They comment that although we 'exist in a world of three-dimensional objects moving through space in regular ways. . . . [How infants and children come to know] the External World is curiously invisible' (Gopnick *et al.* 1999: 60).

The biological aspects of schemas

Our book foregrounds biological processes, in particular the innate drives of pre-school-aged children to learn more through repeating schemes of action that result in cognitive structures about the 'external world'. These cognitive structures – schemas – are arguably the core of developing young minds.

Others have written about what new-born infants already know (for example de Boysson-Bardies 1999; Eliot 1999; Trevarthen 2002). That is not on our agenda. However, their research shows that infants are primed to pay attention to patterns in the material, social and linguistic worlds. Their work confirms that infants are equipped with biological systems for categorization, and can differentiate between patterns (as well as between people). In other words, babies are born with the capacity to develop schemas, and with a motivation to develop them.

Our agenda has been to illustrate how young children work with schemas. Like older humans, they engage in scientific investigations to come to know and understand the material, external world. Children demonstrate an inner drive to seek patterns in phenomena (objects and actions) and use schemas (like young Nina, the spiral spotter). They experiment with making things happen (like young Keir, exploring force and movement). Nina's mother, and the adults in our two research projects, endeavoured to maintain that biologically stimulated motivation to learn, as well as extending the children's experiences and thinking about schemas with relevant content. They helped nature and nurture to 'dance together'.

> The brain [is] shaped by experience and, in turn, . . . this newly remolded brain facilitates the embrace of new experiences, which leads to further neural changes, *ad infinitum*. . . . Experience is responsible for the changes that occur in the brain, which in turn determines the behavioural profile and development of the [child].
>
> (Nelson 1999: 42)

The authors of this book have joined with other researchers – Chris Athey, Cathy Nutbrown and Cath Arnold – who have researched young children's schema development through focusing on forms in figural representation and in actions. In the Competent Children substudy, we focused on children's cognitive structures (neural changes) to do with the external or material world – on schemas associated with natural objects, and schemas seen in cultural artefacts (building structures, vehicles, written symbols, the visual arts, technological outputs, and so on). Most of the schemas studied in early childhood education cluster to develop science or mathematics concepts. Athey's examples ([1990] 2007) of such concepts in her chapter on 'Continuity between Schemas and Concepts' include navigating to find the shortest route on a rail map between A and B, going through boundaries with a magnet, classification of insects and rotation in technological equipment. The exception in her examples is rotation in dance. (Dancers would no doubt verify that dance rotations do necessitate sophisticated physics understanding.)

In the Wilton Playcentre project, the practitioner-researchers continued in that tradition – they too mostly focused on schemas to do with forms in the material world. However, in our continuation of the Wilton Playcentre centre of innovation research, Pam Cubey extended New Zealand schema research: she gathered more data on the links between schema learning and early literacy. Cubey captured examples of children exploring the distinction between patterns in drawing and patterns in writing. Drawing and writing both enrich and extend the ways people communicate with each other. Writing – and reading – are valued more highly for living in our society than art. We too paid particular attention to emergent written literacy, in our case at the Wilton Playcentre children, thereby providing an illustration of what Cathy Nutbrown proposed should happen for early literacy (see her Chapter 6, in the [1994] 2006 edition).

The Wilton Playcentre centre of innovation findings – and our extension study – support Piaget's view that young children's learning progressions involve increasingly comprehensive ways of thinking. Schemas are simple pieces of thought – 'thought foot-stools' (Worthington and Carruthers 2003). The clustering of schemas takes children's thinking on to larger and more complex ideas, for example, into thinking about marks as representations of things.

The role of the subconscious

Schema research in early childhood education reveals how young children are driven by subconscious thought processes for certain aspects of their learning. They are not aware (conscious) of thinking about specific schemas. Understanding human consciousness and the subconscious was – and still is – a new science frontier. Schema learning research provides some insights for scientists, as well as to educationists.

Colwyn Trevarthen talks about aspects of musical (and language) learning being eagerly anticipated by a baby, as seen in his or her initiatives (2002). Nature ensures infants are motivated to engage musically.

I believe we see in infants innate psychological foundations of both musical behaviour and musical awareness that are unique to human beings. A baby's selective orientation to musical sounds, critical discrimination of musical features of sound, and vocal and gestural responses that are timed and expressed to contribute to a joint musical game confirm that music . . . has strong roots in human nature.

(Trevarthen 2002: 21)

Research on oral language development demonstrates parallels (see, for example, the work of de Boysson-Bardies 1999).

The schematic form of thought also has its roots in human nature. There are biological foundations for schematic repeated behaviours and for schema awareness. Toddlers and young children are remarkable in being able to discriminate first between lines and curves and then between different sorts of lines and curves, and in being able to sort out their spatial relationships. Schemas to do with forms – lines, curves, and space orders – like the learning of language and music become cognitively embedded as a consequence of sufficient relevant experience. The cognitive constructs of this sort of learning are stored in implicit memories, in the subconscious systems of the mind.

Trevarthen comments on a 'vitality of awareness' in babies about musical features. In a similar vein, schema researchers on both sides of the globe talk about the intensity of concentration they see when children explore schemas related to science and mathematics; for example, the Wilton Playcentre parents talked about Isabelle and her 'schema face'.

An inner drive motivates children to experiment with categorization until they can readily discriminate between forms. Children perceive different schemas like lines, arcs, zigzags, spirals and enveloping; and then actively explore them through play to develop their knowledge about those forms. That noticing is mostly stored in the subconscious mind; that is, small children are unaware that they are registering the patterns in the physical forms. The same process happens when toddlers register phonemes in spoken language in their subconscious.

Recently, the *New Scientist* published an article focusing on the 'unsung hero of the human mind': subconscious thought processes (Douglas 2007). Its synthesis of research helps to explain what schema researchers have observed; for example, 'Our subconscious is . . . a purposeful, active and independent guide to behaviour' (Douglas 2007: 32).

The article reports that Dehaene's neuroimaging experiments suggest that the subconscious does not function as a separate system from the conscious; they are two parts of the same system. Other points of relevance to those interested in young children's schema learning include:

- when input from the environment becomes important enough, the subconscious decides to engage the conscious;
- conscious and subconscious thought processes work together, each assuming more or less control depending on the situation;
- subconscious thinking is the source of our creative inspiration and is important for factual memory too;
- from about age 8 years, we seem to lose some subconscious ability; for example, the subconscious ability to learn languages efficiently.

When adults recognize and acknowledge a child's schema fascination, the child is assisted to become conscious of it such that they form explicit memories about activities and content associated with their schemas. Keir's interest in volcanoes was strengthened by Sarah making him conscious of his trajectory schema. She created links between his schema interests and content in books and science activities in the sandpit. Similarly, adults helped Nyah become aware of maps as a way of representing her schematic interest in the relationship of different places in the outdoor area of the Playcentre and in the neighbourhood landscape.

We can speculate that when a child talks about actions in relation to his or her schemas, the child's subconscious has engendered consciousness of it.

Schema model of subconscious and consciousness memories

Notwithstanding that learning happens in an individual's mind, learning is greater than an individual matter. Other people are often agents of change in children's (and adults') learning. They are called mediators by socio-cultural theorists (for example Vygotsky). A mediator facilitates the child's development by making it easier for the child to perform certain actions. A mediator extends children's knowledge and deepens their understanding in worthwhile directions. This applies to schema learning as well as content learning.

The effects of mediated schema learning were evident when Chris Athey, researcher, and Tina Bruce, teacher, at the Froebel Institute – and the children's parents – added educative experiences related to schema interests; they found they had grown the children's intelligence. What is the explanation for this?

We have developed a model to show how adult knowledge of schema learning theory and their subsequent interventions to enrich schema understanding makes a significant impact on children's learning (see Figure 6.1). There are three main variables in the model that explain the role of mediators. First, adults who identify schemes of action at play set up iterations between the conscious and the subconscious minds in children by making them conscious of their inner thinking about schemas. Talk is a trigger for the interplay between the subconscious and the conscious minds. To do this effectively, the adults have to know about schemas. As a consequence of adults and children becoming consciously aware, implicit memories became explicit ones where factual memories are formed linked to events and/or content.

Second, the way parents talk *about* their child changes as they share making sense of the world from a child's schematic perspective and, as a consequence, the child's autobiographical narrative memory about their own identity is positively enhanced. That is, children are

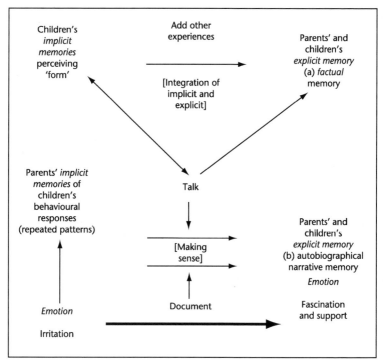

Figure 6.1 Schema learning intervention effects on memories.

portrayed as active learners and thinkers by their parents in ways that enhance children's conceptions of themselves. *Te Whāriki, Early Childhood Curriculum* is introduced by a quote from Donaldson *et al.* (1983: 1) about the significance of the early childhood period, which include phrases such as 'children will form conceptions of themselves . . . as thinkers' and 'reach certain important decisions about their own abilities and their own worth.' Research has shown that parents knowledgeable about their child's schema explorations convey that the child is a thinker, indeed an able thinker.

Third, parents who become knowledgeable about schemas change from being irritated by their child's repetitive behaviours to being fascinated by what they signify for learning – their emotions change. Parents become positively disposed to add support for schema-related learning.

A Wilton Playcentre parent's 2007 'blog' illustrates how knowledge of schemas can moderate an adult's emotional reactions to a child's scheme of actions.

Hazel (a notably clingy child) has just started school. She's doing a lot of disconnecting. She's cutting her bedding, Sean's sock, her teddy's fur. She's been drawing smiles on pieces of paper and cutting them out as presents. She's picking things apart, dismembering dolls and pulling things to pieces. I'm not sure what the content of her stories is; I'm rather worn out with dealing with the physical disconnections. I'm very interested that it is disconnecting that she's doing as she disconnects with us in order to connect with school. (*Susan*)

Our point is that the mother could have reacted to the 'disconnections' with anger. Instead, she said that she was 'interested' (despite being 'worn out').

Children learn through what they do

Schema interests – threads of thought that fascinate young children – differ from adult-initiated themes that are to do with content areas. A schema interest, by definition, is about a form of thought rather than about content.

Self-motivated by their schema interests, children explore commonalities within diverse objects and experiences; they develop their thinking about categories. They also explore the interrelationships of objects. Figurative schema interests lead progressively to understanding symbolic representation – in drawings, constructions and written language. Action schema interests lead progressively to understanding about places and things, such as relationships and orientation of objects in space.

It follows that the environment is very significant for young children's learning. A rich array of diverse objects for them to actively explore is important. Objects in the natural world and cultural artefacts in everyday use have proven their value for centuries.

In the Competent Children sub-study, once the teachers in the schema centres had identified children's schemas, they supplied additional materials so children could further explore different aspects of the schemas in which they were absorbed. This was a very positive pedagogical action. It increased the opportunities for the children to work with and think about schemas that relate to objects. In this way, the teachers assisted children to recognize and competently use schemas to develop their understanding of the natural world. It fostered increasingly comprehensive ways of scientific thinking – say, about gravity – and about concepts in relation to their cultural-historical world, such as neighbourhood landscapes.

The pedagogical approach empowered children to continue taking the initiative in how they would explore schemas. It is also possible that the new materials triggered other children's intellectual curiosity about the same schema.

In most instances, what satisfied the children's intellectual needs was not flash or costly equipment, but simple goods such as sewing tape, cot blankets or cooking ingredients. Often they were used by the children in ways that would not have occurred to adults:

- When Jan and Sam were exploring 'connection', materials they used at home and/or in the centre included shoe laces, a TV programme on trains, pegs, video cases, planks and ladders in the outdoor area, a Duplo train, building blocks, a rod and line (made of sticks and wool), and rope.
- When Paul was exploring 'circular enclosure', 'core and radial', and 'dynamic circular' schemas, the things he was observed using in the centre included tractor tyre, roll of Sellotape™, length of cord, cardboard tube, towelling hair ring, wheel from a toy vehicle, water wheel, lasso, string, ball, scarf, a swing he made himself, cape, pois, paintings, drawings and collage constructions. (Most of these materials were available daily at the centre, although the teachers did supply additional cord, string and rope once they spotted Paul's fascination with tying things about his body; for example, his wrist or waist to experience enclosure. Ready-made equipment, on its own, may not have kept Paul's interest for so long, nor have been so intellectually satisfying.)

Photo 6.1 Coordinator with parent and child.

- The materials *and activities* used by children exploring the 'containing/enveloping' schemas included wrapping blocks and other objects in tissues/paper, folding paintings and other art into parcels with Sellotape™, tucking children into beds, hiding parcels ('presents') under pillows, putting sand in a variety of containers, immersing objects (for example flowers, sponge) in water, making packets of 'fish and chips', sticking decorations all over adults, covering soft toys with fabric, planting 'plants' in the soil outside, putting a plum in a child's mouth, climbing inside items of furniture, putting 'babies' (dolls) inside covered boxes, drawing and painting containers (including one of a teapot with tea coming out of its spout), fitting shapes into a form board, covering bottles of liquid, pouring water over a toy duck, filling containers with water until they overflow and are enveloped by water, tipping out and putting back blocks in a container, playing card games in which pictures are hidden face down, filling sandwiches, and sitting in a cart.

These lists reveal the ingenuity of children in using material and equipment in so many different ways to nourish their understanding of the schemas – and this is only a handful of schemas. (Science – and mathematics-conscious teachers will recognize how many explorations of schemas are, at the same time, experiments about the properties of different materials. They know too that mathematics is a building block of science.)

The conclusion to be drawn, from watching young children play with and learn from objects and materials in ingenious ways, is that if adults structured the programme more or limited the supply of or access to equipment and materials, then exploration by children would be confined. By structuring is meant when adults introduce limits on the times, spaces and materials available for children to play with and explore.

Time to explore an array of materials and equipment with few adult restrictions as to choice and the ready access to the outdoors – where there were plentiful supplies of additional and natural materials and varying landforms – are cause for celebration.

Simon Nicholson's theory of *loose parts* (1971, cited by Greenman 1998: 154) comes to mind when thinking about environments that enrich and extend children's schema thinking. His theory is simple, yet powerful. The basic tenet is that in any environment, both the possibility of discovery and the degree of creativity are directly proportional to the number and kinds of variables or components ('loose parts') for the construction of ideas in it. To discover the features of 'containment' or other schemas through actions, children need access to lots of loose parts *and* the freedom to explore them through play. Open-ended materials are the epitome of loose parts. Blocks, sand, water, clay, paint and coloured pens 'enable children to represent their real experiences, their ideas and imaginings in different ways' (Nutbrown [1994] 2006: 120). Remember Nina, spiral spotter, in Chapter 1? Nina's mother felt that a spiral not having an end was important; Nina could start from a centre and keep going with it to make a spiral, or transform it as her imagination took over and end up with something else. Open-ended materials similarly have endless possibilities.

Children can do many things with materials with loose parts; they can control their use and be creative. To illustrate, here is a teacher's reflection on two types of marble run in a centre:

> The first is a plastic clip-together run with very limited options. It is compact and, because it is purpose-built, it is convenient. The second is . . . made of varying sized wooden blocks, tends to be large and sprawling once built, but has no defined form so the possibilities are all but endless. The first is seldom if ever requested by children, but the second is used on a daily basis.
>
> The first needs adults to put it together and it is either right or

wrong and provides little scope for exploration of one's own creativity. The second can be, and most often is, created with little or no teacher input. This allows the child to take responsibility for their own learning and exploration . . . as wild as their imagination will allow. It is by having this unlimited scope for exploration that the child is open to ask and explore their own questions about what is possible . . . and build knowledge of marble runs and marble mechanics.

> (Greerton Early Childhood Centre of Innovation,
> personal communication 2007)

Visual arts materials similarly offer children (and adults) unlimited scope for exploring ideas and developing understanding. Creating representations of schemas with visual arts materials is an aspect of developing understandings of the forms being explored in schemes of action. Exploring schemas and creating representations of them merge when children work with the arts, so long as the adults haven't stolen the fun and creativity by making things *for* them. The manufacturer had stolen the creativity from the plastic version of the marble run, described above. Teachers in some settings, unfortunately, 'steal' in this way too by limiting and controlling children's exploration of objects.

Dancing with biology

Nurture interacts with nature. Young children's schema learning is enhanced by interaction with peers and with adults.

Children learning from their peers

In the Competent Children action research, the freedom of the children to learn from materials and equipment alongside and by interacting with their peers was notable. The schema children were seldom alone or passive in relation to their peers. Sometimes the children worked in parallel to one another but, more often, there was direct interaction. Thus, it was highly likely that other children were instrumental in the children advancing their communication skills, and in 'learning strategies for active exploration, thinking, and reasoning' (Goal 3 for the Exploration strand of *Te Whāriki*); in this case, for active exploration and thinking about schemas.

The children in the Wilton Playcentre were also very free to explore. That freedom is part of the Playcentre philosophy, and it also suits the wide age range of children playing together. The researchers could observe children 'come to know' more about the schemas and clusters of schemas that fascinated them in contexts where there was no age segregation. Photos (analysed as data) showed sequences where a younger child observed older children, say, exploring a 'vertical' schema with block constructions one week and the younger child making similar constructions a week later. One parent noted that her daughter watched an older child at the Playcentre and practised his actions at home.

> She will try things out at home before she does them at Playcentre – things [involving enveloping] that she has watched older children doing such as painting her face and arms, and hiding under a towel. 'I'm playing like J' [older child]. (*Parent interview*)

The Wilton Playcentre data suggest that there could also be a cognitive match between children motivated to observe carefully and the children being watched. Moreover, the practitioner-researchers speculated that the cross-age interactions could provoke cognitive 'leaps' for younger children.

> There was a schema-related connection between several of our younger children and their heroes. These little 1- and 2-year-olds were observed to admire and copy the older children with similar schema interests. Shivani greatly admired Josie and both had strong enclosing schema interests. Hazel loved to watch and be with Angus, who was a full 4 years older. Both were interested at the time in transporting. We wonder if under these conditions the younger children can make larger cognitive leaps, by reaching to the level of the older child who can show them through their play how schema learning can be extended. The mixed age range of children attending playcentre is beneficial to these young children.
>
> (van Wijk *et al.* 2006)

Earlier in this chapter, we talked about socially mediated learning. The mediators at the Wilton Playcentre were, at times, older children in the same setting. In the Vygotskian framework, mediators become mental tools. Like other cultural tools, mediators' actions can be appropriated by children (Simmons *et al.* 2007). The Wilton Playcentre data showed younger children appropriated the actions of their older role models. In New Zealand Māori cultural learning, older children have a responsibility for young children (especially siblings). This is known as a *tuakana* and *teina* relationship (see, for example, Tamati 2005).

In England, Chris Athey, Cathy Nutbrown and Cath Arnold found that when children were interested in playing with each other, it was often because there was a cognitive 'match' in terms of schemes of action. They appropriated each other's actions.

Children learning from teachers

When adults identify a schema fascination *and* support and extend it through a nourishing environment and language-mediated experiences, more is learned. Cognitive functioning expands.

Adults with responsibilities for young children's learning and development need to go beyond identifying schemas and adding relevant equipment and resources – they must extend the children's schema experiences, including through talk. While the findings from the Competent Children sub-study demonstrated the value of adding materials and experiences for the children to extend their schema understandings, the Froebel Institute and the Wilton Playcentre showed more comprehensive results when adults talked to children about their schemas as well. In the Froebel and Wilton centres, the adults and children were talking about specific shared interests over time. This is a feature that the Effective Pedagogy research team, based at the University of London, argue is significant for positive cognitive outcomes for children:

> If we consider learning to be the result of a process of cognitive construction, this will only be achieved when it is motivated and involved, and it seems entirely consistent to treat the part played by the effective educator in precisely the same way. The cognitive construction in this case would be mutual where each party engages with the understanding of the other and learning is achieved through a process of reflexive 'co-construction'. . . . Our research has shown positive cognitive outcomes are closely associated with adult–child interactions of this kind that involve some element of 'sustained shared thinking'.
> (Siraj-Blatchford and Sylva 2004: 720)

The research interventions and case studies in Chapters 3, 4 and 5 of our book illustrate the value of adult involvement in extending children's schema learning. Once adults have knowledge of schema learning, they notice children demonstrating a fascination with a schema or cluster of schemas through repeated patterns of actions to do with that schema. Then they can respond in meaningful situations to assist the child to progress their thinking.

Nutbrown ([1994] 2006: 37) summarized Vygotsky's arguments for adult involvement clearly:

> According to Vygotsky every piece of learning had a history, a base on which it was built, beginning before formal education and based on real-life experiences. When we stop to think of formal learning of say, writing, we can often trace early beginnings well before organised learning. This kind of learning occurs when children spend time with adults, working on real situations such as baking, filling the washing machine, gardening and writing birthday cards. Vygotsky regarded the match between a child's learning and his or her developmental level as all important. He suggested that children had two developmental levels, their actual developmental level, what they could actually do independently, and a higher level, that which they may next be able to do. Vygotsky identified the interchange between these two levels as the 'one of proximal development', the difference between what children can do alone and what they can do with help, support and guidance. He argues 'what a child can do with assistance today she will be able to do by herself tomorrow' (Vygotsky, 1978, p. 87). This notion emphasises the important role of the adult in fostering progression in children's thinking: helping children to move forward in, and develop their ideas through, positive and interactive learning encounters between children and adults.

Adult mediation in the Competent Children sub-study

In the Competent Children schema centres, one of the key outcomes of the action research was that adults (teachers, parents and researchers) became far more conscious of children being 'absorbed' or 'fascinated', and respectful of their 'intellectual engagement'. The observational aspect of the research explicitly fostered a consciousness of children's absorption, and the teachers and researchers became more aware of what was going on in children's minds in association with repeated patterns of behaviour. These attitudes were passed on to parents. From the evidence gathered, the effects of these changes in the adults (in behaviour and attitudes) seemed to be significant for the children.

Certain processes tend to be ignored when teachers are planning, implementing and evaluating their curriculum. This seems to be true in relation to adults' interactions with children; for instance, in the Competent Children sub-study adult–child interactions were not recorded in the home books, nor in the action researcher's notes.

Either direct adult mediation of children's learning seldom happened, or it was not deemed important enough to mention in records. Either reason is of concern.

In the time-interval observations, in which the researcher was required to note adult interactions, interactions between teachers and target child were reported in 28 per cent of the observation periods. Most of this interaction was fleeting.

Because the large group size in the schema kindergarten (a common situation in kindergartens since the mid-1990s) stacked the odds against individual children receiving attention, it was decided to report the child observation for the two schema centres separately. The target children in the schema kindergarten were seen to interact with a teacher in only 14 per cent of the observation periods; in the schema childcare centre the figure was 44 per cent. (The childcare centre's organization, as well as the better teacher–child ratio, contributed to these results.)

The contacts between adults and children included a mix of children making a request and receiving an answer, exchanging hugs, and conversations. The centres' statements of philosophy all emphasized the importance of giving children opportunities for learning and the value of play. Staff actions observed during the study indicated that these philosophies were implemented daily. Goal 1 for the Exploration strand in *Te Whāriki* was strongly evident. It states, 'Children will experience an environment where their play is valued as meaningful learning and the importance of spontaneous play is recognised'.

Mediation through dialogue was the area that needed improvement. Conversations were rarely noted during the time-interval observations. In addition, all the qualitative data about the children's schemas indicated that few conversations about schemas took place. Thus, teachers were not helping individual children verbalize their thinking. The larger group sizes in kindergartens mean teachers cannot give much time to individual children. However, the occasions when they helped children, via discussions, 'to develop working theories for making sense of the natural, social, physical, and material worlds' (Goal 4 for the Exploration strand in *Te Whāriki*) were few and far between. Indeed, across all four centres, cognitive language extension was recorded in only 7 per cent of the observation intervals.

Positive differences were noted in the schema centres – the researchers rated the schema centres more highly for adult–child interactions. The schema children engaged in more conversations with their teachers (9 per cent compared with 5 per cent), and requested help more often (6 per cent compared with 3 per cent). These results indicate that the schema-centre teachers had adjusted

Photo 6.2 The freedom of children to learn through play – jump.

their responsiveness and their language behaviour. Nevertheless, there were too few conversations. Note that because there were few such events, it was not possible to measure statistical significance and the differences may be chance ones.

Adult mediation at the Wilton Playcentre

The Wilton Playcentre researchers found that everyday spoken language was the medium most often used to extend and enrich children's schematic experiences, and to scaffold the coordination of schemas seen in their concept development.

The parent educators also chose rhymes and songs relevant to dominant schemes of actions to enrich the children's schema language and understandings. In Chapter 5, there are several mentions of stories being read to the case study children.

Pedagogical discussions – with adults using language quite consciously – helped children to recognize and competently use their schemas in developing understanding of their material and social worlds.

Actions form the processes of reasoning, and it is the actions and interplay between the experience of action and thought that form the basis of the way in which a child constructs a view of the world. Language then serves as a system for representing the world.

(Robson 2006: 14)

Schemes of action signal to educators possible lines of direction for planning in order to extend learn-by-doing experiences. For example, when the Wilton Playcentre parent educators recognized Nyah's interest in places and spatial relationships, they planned possible ways to facilitate sustained conversations about related experiences. Martha brought a treasure story to the Playcentre. This book triggered a long-lasting love of treasure stories in several children. Open-ended questions were asked about maps after reading this book, which led to treasure map activities. Martha played with treasure maps at home with Nyah. At the Playcentre, adults and children of different ages made, buried and found lost treasure together using the maps and vocabulary to do with spatial relations, such as 'below', 'beside' and 'inside' in their discussions. The treasure map literacy and mathematical activities continued over days and weeks.

In the community, Isabelle recognized the purpose of a map and took one from the information centre when the family visited a bush park and 'studied it as she walked'. The children's interest in maps took off in a new direction when the children received a letter from a Playcentre child who had gone to North America. Nyah had a long conversation about how the letter would have travelled from this far away place to the Wilton Playcentre, thinking about the stages and means of its transportation in the abstract. For her, and other children, the letter also motivated an interest in written language.

When the research focus turned to schemas in connection with written language, the research stretched the adults' thinking as well. To begin with, the adults found it hard to distinguish between lines and circles drawn by children because they had a fascination with those schemas, and lines and circles drawn as marks on paper to say something in the way adults use marks on paper for written communication. Both could be said to be schematic actions, but there is a distinction as to purpose – to explore a schema or to make a mark to represent words. Listening intently and participating in children's exploration of mark-making over an extended period of time – at home as well as at Playcentre – enabled the parent educators to notice and recognize when their children worked with clusters of schemas to understand *representation*.

For all six case study children, the child's name was one of the first set of written symbols she or he noticed and recognized as representation – a representation of self. Remember:

> Matthew . . . notices a car number plate, very excited to see an 'M' – 'M' for Mattie; 'M' for me. (*Charles, Matthew's father*)

Remember too:

> Joe [at the magnetic board] is excited when he found those that matched, discussing the letters in his name. . . . [His mother] wrote his name on the computer and stuck it on his bed head as a surprise. He was very pleased to see it and showed each family member. (*Lily, Joe's mother*)

Note the word 'excite' in both these journals. Each child's motivation is high, and learning was enhanced, when parents participated in the learning experiences at a personal level.

After writing the letters in their own name, the children's understanding of written marks became more comprehensive: they wanted adults to add a story to their art and then they made books of their own, like Isabelle's book about moving house and Nyah's book about being on the swing. Adults are necessary partners in early writing experiences, as appreciative audience, and as role models, guides and mentors.

Wilton adults lifted children's understanding of representation and its value when they participated in play. For example, writing, sending and receiving letters became a popular activity when the children received the letter from their friend in the USA. The adults encouraged the activity with sustained conversations, helping some children to make a post box and acting as 'posties' (delivering letters children had written to each other to home letter boxes). The parent educators made it possible for the children's choices of direction to shape the curriculum, and they provided meaningful continuity in their learning between home and the Playcentre. Another example was when Helen introduced greater complexity via the pad and pencil for shopping lists during Kaitlyn's game of shops.

Making a 'profile book' for each child at the Playcentre was also important. As stated in Chapter 2, a socio-cultural approach to assessment has been adopted in New Zealand, where children's learning progressions are captured in scrap- or file-books with text and photos for child, parents and teachers to read and revisit. The parent educators at the Wilton Playcentre invested time regularly in making slide shows of sessions and individual profile books containing Learning Stories (Carr 2001) using a digital camera and their computer. They said both forms of documentation made a big difference for the children – to see themselves in action as competent learners (and for the adults to identify and analyse learning progressions). The profile books are very accessible, and go back and forth between home and the Playcentre. They are a very personal story that children love to 'read' with a friend or family member, reliving their experiences and recalling schema fascinations.

The actions to document learning and to revisit it helped the Wilton children make explicit memories from actions that may have first registered only in the subconscious, and to build positive autobiographical narrative memories of their learning.

In this book, we have used 'dance' as a metaphor. It applies to nurture and nature, and the subconscious and the conscious. We found that noticing and recognizing children's schemas gives educators different and useful knowledge of what children bring to new learning experiences about the material world and about written symbols. This approach helps teachers and learners enhance their ability to 'dance' together.

> There is a great deal of evidence that learning is enhanced when teachers pay attention to the knowledge and beliefs that learners bring to a learning task, use this knowledge as a starting point for new [learning], and monitor students' changing conceptions.
>
> (Bransford *et al.* 2000: 11)

Photo 6.3 Joe and Jamie discuss Joe's profile book.

While the children were able to take control of their own learning, the parent educators noted their changing conceptions and thought about additional information that could help children develop understanding. At times their responses were factual about the material world; at other times their responses were deliberately focused on the cultural world of written literacy; and, generally, the teaching of metacognitive skills was integral. The educators were responding to the three core principles of learning (Bransford *et al.* 2000: 21).

Coordination with home and parents

In the Froebel Nursery, all the adults watched and listened with ever-increasing interest to what the children said and did as the patterns in their thinking became apparent through the research. Chris Athey observed, 'Nothing gets under a parent's skin more quickly and more permanently than the illumination of his or her own child's behaviour' ([1990] 2007: 209). Parents moved beyond looking for illumination, and joined the 'dance' with their child's schemas. This was a thrill, and they dropped any leanings toward 'drill'.

At the Wilton Playcentre, there was a gradual transfer of responsibility from an 'expert' to a 'novice' new family in relation to schema learning. This was seen in two ways:

- More knowledgeable parent educators passed on their knowledge of schema theory to newcomers with useful illustrations, in the same way that had happened for them a year or so earlier;
- Children unconsciously demonstrated their schematic strategies for learning to learn to the novice adults once the adults tuned in to the theory.

New parents were attracted to the strong Playcentre traditions of operating using schemas.

> Wilton Playcentre parent-educators use schema learning theory as a framework to 'see' and understand children's learning interests. This theory seems to help engage new members with the centre and their parent-education role. . . . Parent-educators could literally see what their child was learning and thinking about because of the schematic patterns in their behaviour, and came to understand that these actions were purposeful.
>
> (van Wijk 2007: 60–1)

The Wilton children were observed with greater intensity than in other schema research projects because of it being participatory action research in a setting where the parents are the educators. Data were gathering at home as well as in the centre. The study illustrates the advantages for the parent and child in the home environment when the parents are involved in their child's early childhood education environment and in parent workshops associated with it:

> I do like watching him play at home by himself – the patterning can be different from what he does at Playcentre. I like the complementary play of the two environments. (*Parent interview*)

> Our house changes as different schemas are explored – chairs are made into houses one day; [another time] they are sides of a tunnel with blankets as the roof . . . (*Parent interview*)

During interviews with Pam Cubey, parents talked about their deeper understanding of their child's learning and the schemas she or he was exploring in relation to the world. They commented that they talked with their children at home in a different way, and found it easier to enrich their play.

> I feel confident that we are feeding his mind, his learning; that we are truly educating him. (*Parent interview*)

These benefits do not only happen in parent cooperative settings. The effective pedagogy intensive case study project team asked questions about the effects of continuity between the centre and home environments (Siraj-Blatchford *et al.* 2003) and found positive outcomes in a private day nursery that had regular learning-focused communication with families. Making reference to related studies, Siraj-Blatchford and colleagues said:

> If we accept that parents provide sensitive socio-culturally 'embedded' learning environments for their children then it is likely to follow that where there is some consensus and consistency in the home and school's approach to children's learning and the curriculum then more effective learning outcomes could be achieved.

> All 14 case studies encouraged parents to read to their children, but in those settings that encouraged continuity of learning between the early years setting and home, children had better cognitive outcomes. . . . The more knowledge the adult has

of the child the better matched their support and the more effective the subsequent learning. . . .

Our findings suggest that where a special relationship in terms of shared educational aims has been developed *with* parents, and pedagogical efforts are made at home, [good] outcomes may be established.

(Siraj-Blatchford *et al.* 2003: 145–6)

Pam Hanna (2006), drawing on Anne Stonehouse, is clear that in early education settings:

a partnership with parents is not the same as parent involvement. Partnership is about parents feel[ing] powerful in and connected to their child's life based on communication that is 'value-added' or more than the essential information exchanges that also need to take place.

(Hanna 2006: 72–3)

It is important that teachers and parents share information about children's learning and recognize they share the educational role.

In New Zealand, the documentation of children's learning, in individual portfolios and in project books and on wall displays, illuminated by images of learning processes, has transformed both conversations between children, teachers and parents, and relationships between teachers and parents. Parents add to and enrich discussions about the aims and processes of learning in the early childhood settings, and act as pedagogues at home.

I found the digital camera made a big difference to my whole attitude to observation . . . I've spotted so many schemas from the photos; I'm a documentation convert now. (*Parent interview, Wilton Playcentre*)

Observing the children at Playcentre started me thinking of the practical ways I could incorporate some at home to keep the flow going with their schemas. I put up a tent, which extends enclosing. (*Parent interview, Wilton Playcentre*)

Progression in thought

The teachers and parent educators in the two research projects made an important shift to focusing on the *forms of children's thinking* – schemas – which puts them ahead of most teachers. By grasping the opportunities created by the action research, the teachers and parents deepened their theoretical knowledge, and this led to profound insights into the children's intellectual development.

In the Competent Children sub-study, the teachers in the schema centres found that including an additional focus on schemas into their observations and profile records of children and making some *curriculum content* adjustments was a challenge. Initially, it was not easy to spot the schemas, until the adults 'shifted gear' and learned to watch for continuities in children's thinking. Parents were a great help in identifying the intellectual interests that were dominating their children's behaviour.

In the Wilton Playcentre study, the parent educators were the children's parents and most could readily identify their child's schema interests. But both teachers and parent educators needed to go further in terms of attending to *progressions* in young children's schema and other learning. There is an unmistakable tendency for teachers to write themselves out of learning processes, when in fact they need to do the opposite in order to be mediators of learning; that is, to educate the children. This is not an argument for teacher control: the children themselves must continue to be empowered to construct their own learning from a rich variety of materials and experiences, but with more intellectually satisfying discussion with adults.

Gill Poplur found that:

> Teachers who could discuss extensions to a child's shown [schema] and negotiate concepts by sensitively challenging them while remaining inside the child's Zone of Proximal Development were scaffolding the child. These teachers were even more effective in using patterns of thinking to extend the child's thinking because they were maintaining the child's interest with dialogue that would be likely to encourage, challenge and sustain curiosity and experimentation. Their actions could be aligned with the skilled, cognitive dance of which Bruner speaks (1983) that enables a teacher to support a 'strong' child.
>
> (Poplur 2004: 121–2)

But first the adults have to be listening carefully to children to find out their working theories. Worthington and Carruthers (2003) did this and found that children gradually advance towards more complex understandings by coordinating schemas in a zigzag fashion. They make connections between schemas to form new ideas (concepts).

By the time children are approaching 5 years of age, they are often experimenting with 'transformations' and 'functional dependency' in relation to *action schemas*, whereas their earlier work on these schemas was at the motor and symbolic representation levels. In the Competent Children action research, there was little indication that teachers were observing these progressions and consciously fostering children moving to higher levels of intellectual development involving abstract thought.

One reason the teachers did not extend children's abstract thinking could have been the limitations of the action research focus, which concentrated on the *forms of children's thinking*. For example, we were simply asking for isolated examples of specific schemas. It would have been valuable to have also requested a series of examples showing progress through the levels of working and understanding those schemas.

Progression in learning involves going broader and, say, seeing similar patterns in new experiences; and it involves dealing with richness and testing what is possible in the face of increasing complexity. Teachers can foster the testing of ideas and help to extend thinking by using 'thinking' words, such as 'predict', 'plan', 'remember', 'depict', and so on (Hanna 2006: 86), and then staying with the ensuing discussion.

Lilian Katz (1994: 201) proposed that quality programmes must be judged in part on the children's subjective experience of the programme. One of the questions she posed for and on behalf of the child was: Do I find most of my experiences satisfying rather than frustrating or confusing? Without discussions with adults about their more advanced levels of work on schemas, children are likely to answer, 'No, I am frustrated.' Teachers should be helping children move up through schema and other progressions. At the higher levels of schema development, this has to involve discussion.

When teachers engage more with children's progressions in thinking, they too gain something. As Burns (1995: 5) states, 'Teachers who do foster children's thinking are likely to feel greater job satisfaction. They will "experience the thrill of planning and facilitating the children's excitement about new revolutionary cognitive discoveries".'

Midway through the Wilton Playcentre centre of innovation study, Anne Meade raised the practitioner researchers' awareness of the importance of studying progressions in learning. They decided to do some case studies (some of which are used in this book). These case studies provoked another important shift in professional learning about children's thinking (that did not occur at all in the Competent Children action research study).

By way of illustration, we will revisit Keir's schematic interest in vertical movement. The Wilton Playcentre parents recognized it and responded with suitable content in natural and man-made materials, in different places and day after day. The adults joined in his learning about volcanoes. That shared learning became progressively more complex over the weeks; for example, most learned the difference between magma and lava. And they enjoyed a variety of volcano-related work. At home, his parents did not join Keir in flinging themselves off the couch, but they understood these sudden forceful movements were related to his current schema interests. An older sister happily engaged with Keir's fantasy play involving erupting volcanoes.

Keir's parents noted these connected interests, their minds engaged. Recognition of his learning and responding to make it more complex was deeply satisfying for this family, as was evidenced in Sarah keeping a comprehensive journal of Keir's learning progressions that all members loved to read and discuss. The Wilton practitioner-researchers found this and other families' journals rich in qualitative data, triggering further cycles of discussion in the Playcentre community.

Conclusion ■

Nutbrown said, 'Thinking teachers are more likely to shape "a curriculum for thinking children" ' ([1994: 119]; 2006). We conclude that engaging parents as partners with teachers in extending children's thinking will ensure a curriculum for thinking children.

Reflective questions ■

Context

1 Discuss Nicholson's theory of 'loose parts' and the importance of the context of early childhood settings for promoting schema learning.

Children learn from what they do

2 Think about the last week in your setting, and recall at least three examples of different children pursuing their schema interests. What range of equipment and resources did each child prefer when intent on exploring their schemas? What equipment and resources could you add to provide fresh encounters that will help consolidate their understanding of these schemas?

Children learn from their peers

3 Review a sample of photos (and video footage, where applicable) of children learning in order to spot the young observers. Discuss what they were learning from their peers and, in the next fortnight, watch for further growth and development to share with colleagues and parents.

Adult mediation

4 For recent schemes of action that you have noticed and recognized, mentally prepare yourself for possible ways of modifying your own behaviour, such as language use, to extend children's schema learning.
5 How often do you engage in 'sustained shared thinking', including conversations, related to a child's schema interests?

Coordination with home and parents

6 What more could be done in your setting to acknowledge that families are resourceful – full of useful ideas about children's thinking that teachers can connect with and capitalize on? How?
7 Reflect on and plan a workshop for parents and the community for sharing information on schema learning that will benefit the child and his or her family.

Thinking together

8 What do you want to contribute to children's progressions in thinking and understanding? How can you improve the effectiveness of your contributions?

Action research

9 What place do you see observation and other data collection and analysis having in your curriculum?

APPENDIX

Child observation schedule

Researcher: _____

1. **Child's ID** _____ 2. **Gender**   (a) male ☐
                                                        (b) female ☐

   Description _____ 3. **Time**   (a) a.m. ☐
                                                        (b) p.m. ☐

4. **Date** _____   5. **ECS ID**

6. **Type** _____   7. **Age Range**   (a) mixed ☐
                                                        (b) preschool ☐

8. **Observation** 1 2 3 4 5   9. **Location**   (a) indoor ☐
                                                        (b) outdoor ☐

10. **Group size and composition**

   (a) Alone   (b) 1 adult (within 1 metre)
   (c) 1 + adult (distant)   (d) More than 1 adult
   (e) With 1 child   (f) With 2–5 children
   (g) With more than 5 children

Target child's competency/behaviour

Examples

CODE MOST COMPLEX BEHAVIOUR SEEN DURING OBSERVATION PERIOD (11 and 12)

11. **Alone**

   (a) Solitary play

(b) Aimless wandering
(c) Observing/listening/onlooker (distant)

12. Contribution: social skills with other children

A. Parallel

(a) _____ Passive
(b) _____ Active

B. Simple (collaborative/interactive)

(a) Shared objects
(b) Couldn't hear

C. Reciprocal (role/action reversal)
D. Pretend play

(a) _____ Cooperative
(b) _____ Complex

13. Exploration

(a) Verbal problem-solving/knowledge seeking
(b) Exploration with materials/problem-solving in play

14. Aggression

(a) Verbal
(b) Physical

15. Contribution: social skills with adults

(a) No interaction
(b) Group level only
(c) Adult unaware/ignores
(d) Interaction is only with the researcher

(ONE-TO-ONE INTERACTION BETWEEN ADULT AND CHILD,
NO: STOP HERE   YES: COMPLETE SECTION BELOW

16. Child → Adult   Examples

(a) Warm physical contact
(b) Short exchange (e. g. greeting)
(c) Conversation
(d) Request for help/info
(e) Rebuffs/rude/ignores
(f) Child responds non-verbally appropriately (this is not child
   adult!)

17. Adult → Child

A. Intensity

(a) Minimal

   (b) Simple/elaborated
   (c) Intense
   (d) Conversation (couldn't hear content)

B. **Physical contact**

   (a) No close contact
   (b) Warm, positive
   (c) Hugs or holds

C. **Intellectual**

   (a) No cognitive language extension
   (b) Cognitive language extension

D. **Tone**

   (a) Positive
   (b) Negative

18. **Brief description of general context and behaviour observed, including any language:**

REFERENCES

Arnold, C. (2003) *Observing Harry: Child Development and Learning 0–5.* Maidenhead: Open University Press.

Athey, C. ([1990] 2007) *Extending Thought in Young Children: A Parent–Teacher Partnership.* London: Paul Chapman.

Barriball, D. (1985) Pre school outdoor play and the development of concepts essential for the foundations of mathematical understanding. Unpublished paper, Wellington, New Zealand.

Bartholomew, L. and Bruce, T. (1993) *Getting to Know You: A Guide to Record-keeping in Early Childhood Education and Care.* Seven Oaks: Hodder & Stoughton.

Bowman, B., Donovan, S. and Burns, M.S. (2000) *Eager to Learn: Educating Our Preschoolers.* Washington, DC: National Academic Press.

Bransford, J.D., Brown, A.L. and Cocking, R.R. (eds) (2000) *How People Learn: Brain, Mind, Experience and School.* Washington, DC: National Academy Press.

Brierley, J. (1987) *Give Me a Child Until He Is Seven: Brain Studies and Early Childhood Education.* London: Falmer.

Bronfenbrenner, U. (1979) *The Ecology of Human Development.* Boston, MA: Harvard University Press.

Bruce, T. (2004) *Developing Learning in Early Childhood.* London: Paul Chapman.

Bruce, T. (2005) *Early Childhood Education*, 2nd edn. Oxford: Hodder Arnold.

Bruner, J. (1971) The growth and structure of skill, in K.J. Connolly (ed.) *Motor Skills in Infancy.* London: Academic Press.

Bulman, R., Cubey, P., Mitchell, L., Wilson, M. and Wilton Playcentre Members (2005) Creating continuity through literacy experiences at Wilton Playcentre, *Early Childhood Folio*, 9: 10–17.

Burns, V. (1995) Assessment and evaluation's role in the cognitive development of young children: can New Zealand do better? Paper presented at the World Congress of OMEP, Yokohama, Japan, 1–4 August.

Carr, M. (2001) *Assessment in Early Childhood Settings: Learning Stories.* London: Paul Chapman.

Catherwood, D. and Boulton-Lewis, G. (eds) (1993) *The Early Years: Development, Learning and Teaching.* Victoria: Australian Council for Educational Research.

de Boysson-Bardies, B. (1999) *How Language Comes to Children: From Birth to Two Years.* Cambridge, MA: The MIT Press.

Department for Children, Schools and Families (2007) *Early Years Foundation Stage: Statutory Framework and Guidance.* DCSF Publications, www.standards.dfes.gov.uk/primary/publications/foundation_stage/eyfs, accessed 29 November 2007.

Department for Employment and Schools (2003) *Birth to Three Matters: A Framework of Support for our Youngest Children.* London: DfES.

DeVries, R. and Kohlberg, L. (1987) *Constructivist Early Education: Overview and Comparison with Other Programs.* Washington, DC: National Association for the Education of Young Children.

Donaldson, M., Grieve, R. and Pratt, C. (1983) *Early Childhood Development and Education: Readings in Psychology.* Oxford: Basil Blackwell.

Douglas, K. (2007) Meet the unsung hero of the human mind: the other you, *New Scientist*, 2632: 32–6.

Eisner, E.W. (1997) Cognition and representation: a way to pursue the American dream?, *Phi Delta Kappan*, 78 (5): 349–53.

Eliot, L. (1999) *What's Going On In There? How the Brain and Mind Develop in the First Five Years of Life.* New York: Bantam.

Ewing, B. (2005) *Rosetta.* London: Time Warner.

Farquhar, S.E. (2003) *Quality Teaching Early Foundations: Best Evidence Synthesis.* Wellington, NZ: Ministry of Education.

Foss, B. (ed.) (1974) *New Perspectives in Child Development.* London: Penguin.

Gardner, H. (1983) *Frames of Mind – The Theory of Multiple Intelligences.* New York: Basic Books.

Gipps, C. (2002) Socio-cultural perspectives on assessment, in G. Wells and G. Claxton (eds) *Learning for Life in the Twenty-first Century.* Oxford: Blackwell.

Gopnick, A., Meltzoff, A.N. and Kuhl, P.K. (1999) *The Scientist in the Crib: Minds, Brains and How Children Learn.* New York: William Morrow & Company.

Greenman, J.T. (1998) *Caring Spaces, Learning Places: Children's Environments that Work.* Redmond, WA: Exchange Press.

Hanna, P. (2006) *Adults and Children Learning Together*. New South Wales: Pademelon.

Harper, S. (2004) Schemas, *Playcentre Journal*, 121: 18–19.

Howes, C. and Gulluzo, M. (1989) Howes peer play scale; code book for developmental changes in response to peers. Unpublished paper, Los Angeles, CA.

Johnston, J. (2005) *Early Explorations in Science*, 2nd edn. Maidenhead: Open University Press.

Katz, L. (1994) Perspectives on the quality of early childhood programs, *Phi Delta Kappan*, 76 (3): 200–205.

Landry, S.H. and Smith, K.E. (2006) The influence of parenting on emerging literacy skills, in D.K. Dickinson and S.B. Neuman (eds) *Handbook of Early Literacy Research*, Vol. 2. New York: The Guilford Press.

Liljegren, K. (n.d.) Spirals are never ending learning, Reggio Emilia Australia, *Information Exchange*, www.reaie.org.au/; keyword search = spirals, accessed 19 May 2007.

McTaggart, P. (1989) Principles for participatory action research. Paper presented at the 3 er Encuentro Mundial Investigacion Participativa (The Third World Encounter on Participatory Research), Manuaga, Nicaragua, September.

Meade, A. (1985) *The Children Can Choose: A Study of Early Childhood Programmes in New Zealand*. Wellington: New Zealand Council for Educational Research.

Meade, A. (1994) 'C' multiplied by 5 = cognitively competent children: some insights from the competent children project. An invited address, Australian Early Childhood Association 20th Triennial Conference, Perth, 17–20 September.

Meade, A. (1996) Schemas: helping children's thinking. Unpublished talk given at an OMEP Manawatu Chapter meeting, Palmerston North, New Zealand, September.

Meade, A. (2001) One hundred billion neurons: how do they become organised?, in T. David (ed.) *Promoting Evidence Based Practice in Early Childhood Education: Research and its Implications. Advanced Applied Early Childhood Education*, Vol. 1. Oxford: Elsevier Science.

Meade, A. (ed.) (2007) *Cresting the Waves: Innovation in Early Childhood Education*. Wellington, NZ: NZCER Press.

Ministry of Education (1995). *Beginning School Mathematics Evaluation*. Wellington: author.

Ministry of Education (1996) *Te Whāriki: He Whāriki Mātauranga Mō Ngā Mokopuna o Aotearoa; Early Childhood Curriculum*. Wellington, New Zealand: Learning Media.

Ministry of Education (2002) *Pathways to the Future/Nga Huarahi*

Arataki: A 10-year Plan for Early Childhood Education. Wellington, NZ: author.

Ministry of Education (2004) Socio-cultural assessment/he Aromata-wai Ahurea Paapori, in *Kei tua o te Pae/assessment for Learning: Early Childhood Exemplars*. Wellington, NZ: author.

Mitchell, L. and Cubey, P., with Engelbrecht, L., Lock, M., Lowe, J. and van Wijk, N. (2004) *Wilton Playcentre: A Journey of Discovery, the Beginning*. Wellington: New Zealand Council for Educational Research.

Moyles, J. (1989) *Just Playing? The Role and Status of Play in Early Childhood Education*. Buckingham: Open University Press.

Neisser, U. (1976) *Cognition and Reality*. San Francisco, CA: W.H. Freeman.

Nelson, C. (1999) Neural plasticity and human development, *Current Directions in Psychological Science*, 8 (2): 42–5.

Nutbrown, C. ([1994] 2006) *Threads of Thinking: Young Children Learning and the Role of Early Childhood*. London: Paul Chapman.

Nuthall, G. (2007) *The Hidden Lives of Learners*. Wellington: NZCER Press.

Osborne, R. (1985) Assumptions about teaching and learning, in R. Osborne and P. Freyberg (eds) *Learning in Science: The Implications of Children's Science*. Auckland: Heinemann.

Phillips, G., McNaughton, S., Macdonald, S. and Keith, M. (2002) *Picking Up the Pace: A Summary*. Wellington, NZ: Ministry of Education.

Piaget, J. (1959) *The Construction of Reality in the Child*. New York, NY: Basic Books.

Piaget, J. (1962) *Play, Dreams and Imitation in Childhood*. London: Routledge & Kegan Paul.

Podmore, V., May, H. and Carr, M., with Cubey, P., Hatherly, A. and Macartney, B. (2000) *The Child's Questions: Programme Evaluation with Te Whāriki Using 'Teaching Stories'*. Wellington: Institute for Early Childhood Studies, Victoria University of Wellington.

Poplur, G. (2004) Early childhood teachers' use of schemas in practice. Unpublished MEd thesis, University of Auckland, New Zealand.

Qualifications and Curriculum Authority, and Department for Education and Employment (2000) *Curriculum Guidance for the Foundation Stage*. London: QCA and DfEE.

Ramsey, K., Breen, J., Sturm, J., Lee, W. and Carr, M. (2006), in A. Meade (ed.) *Riding the Waves: Innovation in Early Childhood Education*. Wellington, NZ: NZCER Press.

Ridley, K. (2007) Thinking skills in the early years: a literature review, *Research Information for Teachers*, 1: 12–14.

Robson, S. (2006) *Developing Thinking and Understanding in Young Children: An Introduction for Students*. Oxford: Routledge.

Rogoff, B. (2003) *The Cultural Nature of Learning*. Oxford: Oxford University Press.

Roskos, K., with Hanbali, O. M. (*c.* 2002) *Creating connections, building constructions: Language, literacy and play in early childhood; an invited commentary*, www.readingonline.org/articles/roskos/article.html, accessed 30 August 2007

Schweinhart, L.J. and Weikart, D. (1986) Three preschool curriculum models: academic and social outcomes, *Principal*, 66 (1), 62–4, 67–8.

Siegler, R.S. (2000) The rebirth of children's learning, *Child Development*, 71 (1): 26–35.

Simmons, H., Schimanski, L., McGarva, P., Haworth, P. and Cullen, J. (2007) A bilingual intercultural setting – what have we discovered?, in A. Meade (ed.) *Cresting the Waves: Innovation in Early Childhood Education*. Wellington, NZ: NZCER Press.

Siraj-Blatchford, I., Sylva, K., Taggart, B., Sammons, P., Melhuish, E. and Elliot, K. (2003) *Intensive Case Studies of Practice Across the Foundation Stage, EPPE Technical Paper 10*. London: Institute of Education, University of London.

Siraj-Blatchford, I. and Sylva, K. (2004) Researching pedagogies in English pre-schools, *British Educational Research Journal*, 30 (5): 713–30.

Snow, C.E., Burns, M.S. and Griffin, P. (eds) (1998) *Preventing Reading Difficulties in Young Children*. Washington, DC: Department of Education.

Squire, L.R. (1995) Memory and brain systems, in R. Broadwell (ed.) *Neuroscience, Memory and Language: Decade of the Brain*, Vol. 1. Washington, DC: US Government Printing Office.

Tamati, A. (2005) 'Ma tōu rourou, ma tōku rourou.' The concept of Ako: co-construction of knowledge from a kaupapa Māori perspective, *Early Education*, 37: 23–31.

Tishman, S. (1994) What makes a good thinker? A look at thinking dispositions, *Harvard Graduate School of Education Alumni Bulletin*, 7, 11–14.

Tizard, B. and Hughes, M. (1984) *Young Children Learning: Talking and Thinking at Home and School*. London: Fontana.

Trevarthen, C. (2002) Origins of musical identity: evidence from infancy for musical social awareness, in R.A.R. Macdonald, D.J. Hargreaves and D. Miell (eds) *Musical Identities*. Oxford: Oxford University Press.

van Wijk, N., Simmonds, A., Cubey, P. and Mitchell, L., with Bulman, R., Wilson, M. and Wilton Playcentre members (2006) *Transforming Learning at Wilton Playcentre*. Wellington: New Zealand Council for Educational Research.

van Wijk, N., with the Wilton Playcentre community (2007) Wilton

Playcentre: a community of learners, tall and short, in A. Meade (ed.) *Cresting the Waves: Innovation in Early Childhood Education*. Wellington, New Zealand: NZCER Press.

Videatives Views (2007) Are they talking? *Issue 38*. Retrieved 20/7/07.

Vygotsky, L. (1978) *Mind in Society*. Cambridge, MA: Harvard University Press.

Whalley, M. (2000) Parents' involvement in their children's learning, *Early Childhood Practice*, 2 (1): 36–57.

Whitehead, M. (2001) *The Development of Language and Literacy*. London: Paul Chapman/Sage.

Wilson, M. and Bulman, R., with van Wijk, N., Engelbrecht, L., Schuker, C., Cubey, P., and Mitchell, L. (2005) An action research cycle on literacy, mark-making and numeracy and the use of open-ended questions. Unpublished paper, Wilton Playcentre, Wellington.

Wilton Playcentre members, with Cubey, P. and Mitchell, L. (2005) Innovation at Wilton Playcentre, in A. Meade (ed.) *Catching the Waves: Innovation in Early Childhood Education*. Wellington, NZ: NZCER Press.

Worthington, M. (published as Hayton) (1996) Emergent and developmentally appropriate learning: the relationship to personal views of learning. *Primary Practice*, 5: 16–17.

Worthington, M. and Carruthers, E. (2003) *Children's Mathematics: Making Marks, Making Meaning*. London: Paul Chapman.

Wylie, C. (1996) *Five Years Old and Competent*. Wellington: New Zealand Council for Educational Research.

Wylie, C. (1999) *Eight Years Old and Competent*. Wellington: New Zealand Council for Educational Research.

Wylie, C. (2004) *Twelve Years Old and Competent*. Wellington: New Zealand Council for Educational Research.

INDEX

Locators shown in *italics* refer to figures and photos.

EARLY YEARS FOUNDATIONS
MEETING THE CHALLENGE

Janet Moyles

With so many challenges facing early years professionals, there are continual dilemmas arising between doing what one knows is essentially 'right' for birth-to-five-year-olds from all backgrounds and conforming to the demands made by government and policy makers. This exciting and original book supports practitioners in thinking through their roles to meet some of the many issues they encounter.

Using the new *Early Years Foundation Stage* principles as its framework, the contributors support early years professionals in dealing with issues and challenges in a sensitive and professional manner, with particular emphasis upon the need for practitioners to personalise the requirements for each child in their care and to reflect closely upon their own and children's experiences.

Topics include: the changing landscape of early childhood, culture, identity and diversity, supporting playful learning, outdoor learning, documenting children's experiences, developing independence in learning, the meaning of being creative, play and mark-making in maths, and literacy.

Each section is introduced with some background research and information to provide evidence and guidance upon which practitioners can make their own decisions. Individual chapters include questions for reflection, points for discussion and suggestions for additional reading.

Contents
Notes on contributors – Introduction – Changing the landscape of early childhood – Section one: A unique child – Introduction – Primary communication: What can adults learn from babies? – Difference, culture and diversity: Challenges, responsibilities and opportunities – Identity and children as learners – Section two: Positive relationships – Introduction – Working together to support playful learning and transition – Somebody else's business: A parent's view of childhood – Coping with bereavement – Vision, mission, method: Challenges and issues in developing the role of the early years mentor teacher – Birth-to-three: The need for a loving and educated workforce – Section three: Enabling Environments – Introduction – The challenges of starting school – Children's outdoor experiences: A sense of adventure? – Written observations or walks in the park? Documenting children's experience – Food for thought: The importance of food and eating in early childhood practice – Section four: Learning and development – Introduction – Developing independence in learning – What does it mean to be creative? – Multimodality, play and children's mark-making in maths – 'Hi Granny! I'm writing a novel.' Literacy in early childhood: Joys, issues and challenges – Endpiece – Appendix – Index.

2007   308pp
978–0–335–22349–7 (Paperback)   978–0–335–22348–0 (Hardback)

DEVELOPING REFLECTIVE PRACTICE IN THE EARLY YEARS

Alice Paige-Smith and Anna Craft (eds)

Reflective practice is a vital aspect of working with young children and enables a deeper understanding of their learning and development. Whilst there is a long tradition among early childhood practitioners of closely observing children's learning so as to nurture and stimulate their development, they are increasingly expected to reflect on their own practice in a variety of ways, in order to enhance their professional development and improve their practice.

This book supports early years practitioners in articulating and understanding their own practice in greater depth, exploring some ways in which they can be encouraged to engage in reflecting on their practice. The book will help early years practitioners develop their reflective skills, enabling them to confidently articulate their practice, values and beliefs.

It offers opportunities to reflect on how theory, research and policy relate to distinct understandings of children's development and learning. By exploring different ways of understanding their own practice and linking this with theory and policy, practitioners are enabled to think about ways of improving their practice.

Developing Reflective Practice in the Early Years is essential reading for all early years practitioners working in early years settings for children aged 0-8 years, including nurseries, children's centres and schools.

Contributors
Naima Browne, Anna Craft, Michael Craft, Caroline Jones, Alice Paige-Smith, Linda Pound, Michael Reed, Jonathan Rix, Elizabeth Wood.

Contents
List of figures – Notes on the contributors – Foreword – Acknowledgements – Introduction – Part 1: What does being a reflective early years practitioner involve? – Introduction to Part 1 – What does it mean to reflect on our practice? – Developing reflective practice – Exploring leadership: The roles and responsibilities of the early years professional – Part 2: How does reflective practice inform work with children? – Introduction to Part 2 – Children's social and emotional development – Inclusion and early years settings: What's your attitude? – Creativity and early years settings – Listening to young children: Multiple voices, meanings and understandings – Part 3: Leading edge practice: A community of reflective professionals – Introduction to Part 3 – Multi-agency working: Rhetoric or reality? – Reflective family-centred practices: Parents' perspectives and early intervention – Professional development through reflective practice – Reflection and developing a community of practice – Postscript: Democratic reflective practice in the early years.

2007 216pp
978–0–335–22277–3 (Paperback)   978–0–335–22278–0 (Hardback)

CHILD DEVELOPMENT FROM BIRTH TO EIGHT
A JOURNEY THROUGH THE EARLY YEARS

Maria Robinson

Understanding child development is crucial for all early years practitioners and a sound knowledge of children and their development underpins effective practice.

The book presents a detailed and in-depth picture of early years development, particularly of developmental processes and interactions. Rather than focusing on a particular topic, it offers a broad overview from a range of sources including:

- Developmental, evolutionary and cognitive psychology
- Biology
- Sensory information
- Attachment theory
- Neuroscience
- Research linking brain function and emotions

As well as providing a great insight into the aspects of child development and offering the benefits of a multi-disciplinary approach, the book emphasizes appropriate pedagogical approaches and the implications for adults who work with young children.

Child Development from Birth to Eight is essential reading for all early years students and practitioners.

Contents
Foreword – Acknowledgements – Introduction – Laying the foundations: Brain works – 'A world of one's own': The body and the senses – Origins – Emotional and social and well being – Learning and development – Playing and imagining – The role of the adult: To understand the 'heart of the intended communication' – The final phase, conclusions and reflections on development – Appendix – Glossary – Notes – Bibliography – Index.

2007   584pp
978–0–335–22097–7 (Paperback)   978–0–335–22098–4 (Hardback)